Regina's seasonal table
recipes to savor
throughout the year

By Chef Regina Mehallick, **R bistro**

dine

Text copyright © 2008 by
Regina Mehallick
Photography copyright © 2008 by
Northstar Media, LLC d/b/a
Indianapolis dine magazine

Library of Congress Catalog-in-
Publication Data available.

ISBN-13: 978-0-9820296-0-2

Manufactured in the USA

10 9 8 7 6 5 4 3 2 1

Northstar Media, LLC
120 East Vermont Street
Indianapolis, IN 46204

www.indianapolisdine.com

contents

introduction

When I started using cookbooks, long before I attended culinary school or even dreamed of opening my own restaurant, I followed recipes to a "T." If it called for ¼ teaspoon salt, I used exactly ¼ teaspoon salt, never deviating from the recipe in any way. In culinary school, I learned to be more free-spirited. I played it loosey-goosey all the time, and dishes still turned out delicious. I started to trust myself, moving through the kitchen and the cooking process by feel rather than formula.

Since then, I've taken classes for fun, worked in kitchens in America, England and Scotland under a number of talented chefs, and found a home in Indianapolis. Since 2001, I've

been cooking in my own restaurant kitchen at R bistro. With a menu that changes weekly and seasons that offer us a rotating bounty of fresh goods, I continue to experiment, and to be surprised and excited by the tastes I create.

Much of what I've learned is found in this book. These so-called lessons aren't rules or technical cooking methods. They're reflections of the foods that I truly enjoy. You'll find traces of my experiences in Glasgow, where local seafood in Scotland was tinged with South American and Thai flavors. You'll also notice a cooking style I developed during my three years in England, where my appreciation of establishing balance on the plate took hold. But perhaps mostly you'll recognize the bountiful flavors of Midwestern USA from R bistro, the seasonal table where I spend most of my time and creative energy. I hope you will enjoy these dishes as much as I do. Happy cooking.

balance and variety

Many cookbooks organize recipes by course (appetizer, entree, dessert) or dish type (pork, vegetables, pastries). Too often this is based on the notion that a plate is composed essentially of a large serving of protein with a starch and vegetable playing second fiddle. But creating meals shouldn't be a fill-in-the-blanks exercise. The protein — always cooked correctly — generally only needs to be about 4-6 ounces. Accompaniments such as a vegetable and starch are served to enhance the entire dining experience, not just the protein. The plate as a whole should exhibit a mix of textures, colors, aromas and temperatures. This style of cooking doesn't require a lot of exotic ingredients, just a variety of ingredients that work well together.

seasonal and local

Before I opened R bistro, I planned to some day have my own little gourmet store. I love visiting these kinds of shops and markets, especially in other cities, and finding those delicious little gems that define a place. I think it was my habit of treating food as souvenirs that interested me most. During our regular visits to Pittsburgh, my husband Jim and I always find our way to Italian market Pennsylvania Macaroni Co. — Penn Mac to the locals — with its incredible selection of cheeses and pastas. There's a spice store in Saint Augustine, Florida, that can't be missed, and Charleston beckons with its creamy grits.

In Indianapolis, I treat my ingredients the same way. For years, I've worked with our area's wonderful farmers to find those seasonal, just-picked berries, tender lamb and fresh lettuce leaves used in my restaurant. Like the souvenir foods in other parts of the country, our local foods tell a story of changing seasons. Eating seasonally and locally can make cooking and entertaining more meaningful, filled with the rich flavors of the freshest foods. Consequently, I've organized the chapters of *Regina's Seasonal Table* by season. I encourage you to cook within each chapter, seeking out those beloved Indiana products or adapting the dishes to take advantage of what's just picked and delicious in your own community.

recipe structure

Many of my dishes, such as Marinated lamb T-bones with Himalayan red rice and sauteed broccoli rabe (page 23) and Chicken breast topped with warm mushrooms, leeks and goat cheese over dressed mixed greens (page 77), include three or four parts. These complete recipes make up the kind of delicious, structured plate I appreciate, but they should also engender creativity. You should feel comfortable mixing and matching the parts to create your own combinations of flavors and textures. Try using a chicken marinade for lamb; opt for couscous instead of quinoa; borrow a salad dressing from another recipe to dress leaves; or substitute your garden's fresh vegetables into a summer toss recipe. Don't be afraid to stray from a recipe and exercise some freedom in the kitchen.

using what works

In my nonprofessional cooking life, I was always gathering recipes — which I still do, including a collection of close to 400 cookbooks — and searching for the perfect version of a recipe. What I've learned is that if you've found a basic technique that works well, stop looking for a better way to do it. My piecrust recipe hasn't changed in years, and it probably never will. It never fails, and it's delicious. If it works, stick with it.

a few basic techniques

Though it has its place in any good cook's canon, *Regina's Seasonal Table* is not a guide to basic preparation and cooking methods. A reference-type cookbook should always be handy to teach and remind us how to accomplish fundamental techniques. For years, I turned to the *Betty Crocker Cookbook* to make no-fail jelly roll cakes and beef goulash. My mother, a consummate baker, trusted Lily Haxworth Wallace's wildly popular *The New American Cookbook,* published in 1941. These days, I keep a copy of Irma S. Rombauer's *Joy of Cooking* in my office at R bistro. With simple illustrations and comprehensive descriptions, it is a great book to explain everything from cleaning fish to icing cakes.

One other indispensable piece of equipment is an instant-read thermometer. Using one is the best way to ensure protein is cooked correctly. Simply insert it into the thickest part of the meat to get a proper reading. Carryover cooking that takes place after meat is removed from the oven will increase its temperature up to 10 degrees. Therefore, plan on pulling the meat out of the oven when the meat is 5-10 degrees shy of its target temperature. Here are some simple guidelines to follow.

internal temperatures for cooking meat

Ground beef, veal, lamb and pork: 160 degrees

Beef, veal, lamb (roasts, steaks, chops)
Rare: 120-125 degrees
Medium-rare: 130-135 degrees
Medium: 140-145 degrees
Well-done: 160 degrees

Chicken and duck: 160 degrees

Pork (roasts, steaks, chops)
Medium: 140-145 degrees
Well-done: 160 degrees

Ham, uncooked: 160 degrees
Ham, fully cooked, reheat: 140-145 degrees

Fish (steaks, filleted or whole): 140 degrees

spring

Though January is the first month of our calendar year, spring feels like the actual beginning. This is when we as cooks and food lovers emerge from long days of cold and dampness with eager anticipation.

The promise of local leaves and lamb, rumors of crisp asparagus and a veritable explosion of young vegetables rouse our winter-weary palates. The dishes we make and enjoy should be just as stirring.

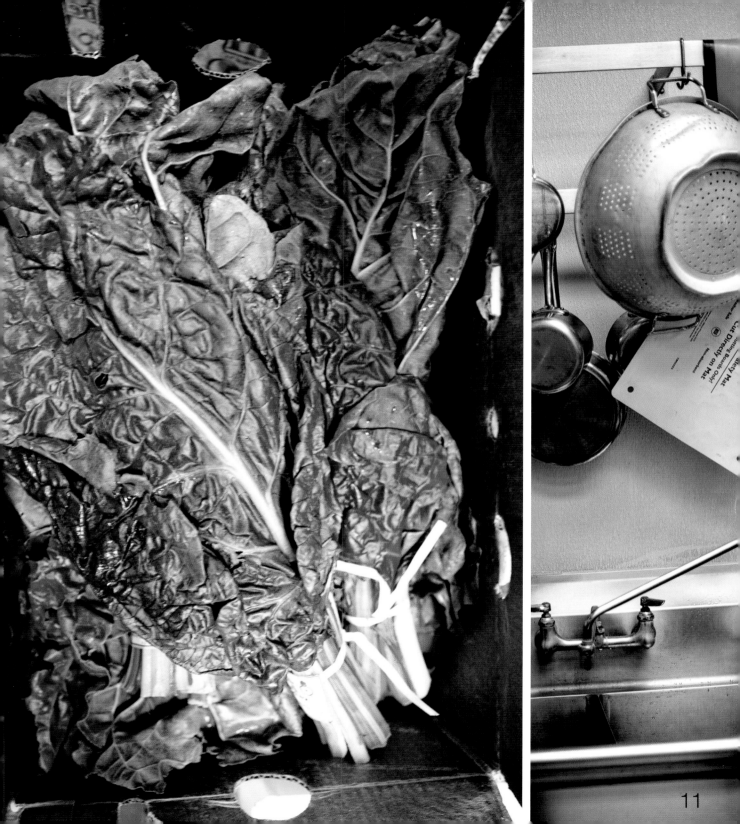

"The asparagus, roasted peppers, dressing, olive

Asparagus, red pepper and goat cheese salad

I recall finding a version of this recipe in *Bon Appétit* magazine several years ago. I have used it as a lunch entree with mixed leaves as a base, but I've also served it as a first course dish in which the asparagus, roasted peppers, dressing, olives and goat cheese make up a perfect spring plate.

white wine vinaigrette

2 tablespoons white wine vinegar
2 tablespoons drained capers
1 tablespoon Dijon mustard
2 teaspoons chopped tarragon
1 clove garlic, finely chopped
½ small red onion, finely chopped
Kosher salt and freshly ground black pepper, to taste
¼ cup plus 2 tablespoons extra-virgin olive oil

1. Combine all of the dressing ingredients except oil in a large bowl.

2. Whisk together the dressing and then slowly whisk in the oil. Correct seasoning, to taste.

vegetables

Kosher salt, to taste
1 pound asparagus (5-7 spears per person)
1 red pepper
Extra-virgin olive oil, as needed

1. In a large pot of boiling salted water, blanch the asparagus just until tender. This could be a short time (about 2 minutes), so don't leave the pot. Remove the spears and immediately plunge into an ice water bath to stop the cooking process. Drain and pat dry.

2. Preheat oven to 400 degrees.

3. Rub the pepper with oil and place it on a sheet pan. Roast in the 400-degree oven 15-25 minutes, turning as it browns and blisters. Remove and place in a bowl; cover with plastic wrap and let it cool.

4. When it is cool, remove the skin, seeds and stems; cut it into strips.

assembly

12 kalamata olives, pitted and halved
4 ounces goat cheese, crumbled

1. Toss the asparagus in a little white wine vinaigrette and divide among 4 salad plates.

2. Toss the peppers and olives in the dressing and place a small bundle in the center of the asparagus.

3. Garnish with the crumbled goat cheese. Drizzle with additional dressing on the asparagus and plate. (As an alternative presentation, serve the vegetables on a base of mixed greens and place the olives alongside the vegetables, as shown in the photo on page 12.)

Serves 4

Prosciutto de Parma over a salad of mango, cucumber and fennel

Classically, Parma ham is served with cantaloupe or figs. This is a different version with a chilled salad of mango, strawberry, cucumber and fennel. It creates a beautiful plate that tastes delicious — with elements of sweetness and saltiness — and has a creamy texture.

salad

1 mango, peeled, seeded and chopped
1 pint strawberries, sliced
1 English cucumber, partially peeled, seeded and chopped
1 head fennel, core removed and bulb chopped;
 fronds chopped
1 bunch chives, chopped
1 teaspoon orange zest
Juice of 2 oranges
2 tablespoons extra-virgin olive oil
1 pinch ground cardamom
Kosher salt and freshly ground black pepper, to taste
Sugar, to taste

1. Toss all of the prepared fruits and vegetables with the remaining ingredients and adjust with seasonings, to taste.

assembly

12 paper-thin slices prosciutto de Parma
Extra-virgin olive oil, as needed

1. Scatter the salad among 4 plates. Top each with 3 slices prosciutto. Drizzle with olive oil.

Serves 4

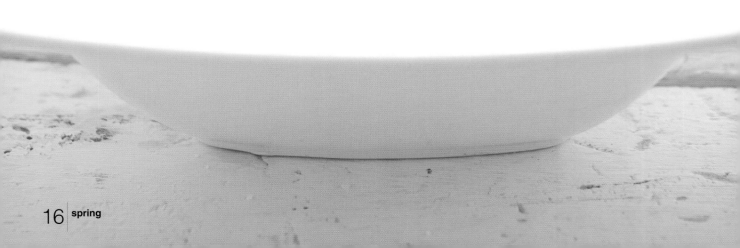

Pasta primavera

This is my version of a pasta primavera. It includes a colorful variety of produce great for spring. Blanching the vegetables is key to retaining their vivid colors and flavors.

1 pound penne pasta
Kosher salt, to taste
1 drizzle plus 2 tablespoons extra-virgin olive oil
1 cup broccoli flowerets
1 cup cauliflower cut into flowerets
½ cup green beans cut into 2-inch pieces
2 carrots, diced
1 clove garlic, minced
1 pinch red pepper flakes
½ cup peas
½ cup mushrooms, sliced
2 large tomatoes, skinned, seeded and chopped
Fresh parsley, chopped, to taste
Fresh basil, chopped, to taste
Fresh thyme, chopped, to taste
Fresh oregano, chopped, to taste
Vegetable stock, as needed
1 cup spinach chiffonade (cut into ribbon-like strips)
Freshly ground black pepper, to taste
Grated Parmesan cheese, to taste

1. Cook the penne in boiling salted water until al dente (according to package directions). Remove from heat, drain the pasta and then return the pasta to the pot, stirring with a drizzle of olive oil to keep it from sticking. Set aside.

2. Bring a pot of salted water to a boil over high heat. Drop the broccoli into the boiling water to blanch (1 minute). Scoop out the broccoli and immediately plunge it into ice water to stop the cooking process. Drain well and set aside. Follow the same procedure for the cauliflower, green beans and carrots, in the same water in separate batches, being careful not to overcook the vegetables.

3. To prepare the sauce, heat the 2 tablespoons oil in a large skillet over medium-high heat and add the minced garlic and red pepper flakes, being careful not to let these burn. Add the broccoli, cauliflower, beans, carrots, peas and mushrooms and stir until crispy tender for at least 2½-3½ minutes.

4. Add the tomatoes and herbs. Simmer until the tomatoes are tender but remain somewhat firm (1-2 minutes).

5. To the skillet, add the pasta with a little vegetable stock, as needed, to adjust consistency; add the spinach, tossing until just wilted.

6. Season generously with salt and pepper, adjusting to taste. Toss with Parmesan cheese, to taste. Serve in individual pasta bowls with more Parmesan and chopped parsley, to garnish.

Serves 6

Italian chicken cutlet with orzo and broccoli

This is a combination of ideas. The chicken cutlet is how I've been preparing breaded chicken at home for years. Just a little of this and that, but the outcome is pure flavor and moistness. Snagged from one of my Italian cookbooks, the broccoli recipe turned out to be fairly easy and loaded with flavor. It adds beautiful color to the plate. This orzo salad is a combination of things I thought would go well together, and that hunch has turned out to be true. We've had this on the menu at R bistro several times with success.

Italian chicken

½ cup flour
Kosher salt and freshly ground black pepper, to taste
2 eggs, gently whisked
1 tablespoon water
½ cup dry bread crumbs
2 teaspoons dried Italian seasoning (such as McCormick or grocery store brand)
¼ cup grated Parmesan cheese
1 pinch garlic powder
4 6-ounce chicken breasts, pounded to an even thickness (not totally flattened, try to keep the shape)
Vegetable oil, as needed

1. Prepare a breading station. To do so, set up 3 shallow bowls in a row. In the first bowl, place the flour and season with salt and pepper, to taste; toss to distribute. In the next bowl, gently whisk the eggs and water. In the third bowl, combine the bread crumbs, Italian seasoning, Parmesan cheese and garlic powder.

2. Coat a flattened chicken breast with flour; shake off any excess. Place it in the egg mixture, being sure that the entire breast is coated. Gently place it in the crumb mixture and cover entirely, turning and pressing to be sure it's nicely coated. Repeat for each breast.

3. Preheat oven to 375 degrees.

4. Heat a generous drizzle of oil in a large skillet or saute pan over medium-high heat, swirling the skillet to coat the bottom. Pan saute the breasts, cooking on one side just until golden brown and then turning them over and cooking the other side until golden brown. Once you've browned both sides, place the chicken on a sheet pan and finish in the 375-degree oven (3-5 minutes).

broccoli in lemon and red chili pepper

¼ cup extra-virgin olive oil, plus more to serve
1 small fresh red chili pepper, seeds removed and finely chopped, or ½ teaspoon crushed dried red chili pepper
3 canned flat anchovy filets
Kosher salt, to taste
1 bunch broccoli (about 1½ pounds)
Juice of ½ lemon (about 2 tablespoons)
Freshly ground black pepper, to taste

1. To make the dressing, put the olive oil, chili pepper and anchovies in a small saute pan. Heat the oil until it is just warm, and the anchovies melt. Turn off the heat and set aside until needed.

2. Bring a pot of salted water to a boil over high heat. Trim the tough ends of the broccoli. Peel the stalks with a paring knife. Separate the broccoli flowerets into generous pieces. Julienne the stalks so that they are about the same size as the flowerets. Cook the broccoli (stalks and flowerets) in the boiling water until it is bright green and tender but still crisp (about 3 minutes). Drain the broccoli and refresh in ice water until cold; drain well.

3. To serve, reheat the broccoli in a pan with a dash of olive oil. Add some of the dressing to flavor the broccoli and then season with salt and pepper, to taste.

warm orzo salad

1 pound orzo pasta
Kosher salt, to taste
½ cup pine nuts
½ cup shelled pistachios
1 tablespoon extra-virgin olive oil, plus more as needed
1 fennel bulb, small dice; reserve the fronds and chop,
  to garnish
3 stalks celery, small dice
Freshly ground black pepper, to taste
½ bunch Italian flat-leaf parsley, chopped
1 cup currants (or white raisins)
1 bunch green onions, chopped (green parts only)
Freshly squeezed orange juice, to taste

1. Cook the orzo in boiling salted water until it's al dente (according to package directions).

2. Preheat oven to 400 degrees.

3. Place the pine nuts and pistachios on 2 small sheet trays. Toast the nuts in the 400-degree oven until golden. (They will brown at their own rates. Check after 3 minutes and watch carefully until lightly toasted.) Remove from the oven and allow to cool. Roughly chop the pistachios.

4. In a large saute pan over medium heat, add 1 tablespoon oil; swirl to coat the bottom of the pan. Add the diced fennel and celery and saute until tender. Season with salt and pepper, to taste. Remove from heat and allow to cool.

5. Toss the orzo, pine nuts, pistachios, diced fennel, celery, parsley, currants, green onions and about ¾ of the fennel fronds with a little olive oil to keep the orzo from sticking. Add the orange juice and season with salt and pepper, to taste.

6. Serve at room temperature, being sure to mix thoroughly.

assembly

1. Spoon portions of warm orzo salad onto 4 plates (save the extra for a snack). Arrange the broccoli in lemon and red chili pepper to the side of the salad and the Italian chicken on top. Garnish with chopped fennel fronds. (An alternative presentation appears in the photo below.)

Serves 4

Turkey meatloaf with leek mash and green beans

I've been making this turkey meatloaf since the early '90s. I adapted the recipe from one that appeared in *Bon Appétit* magazine and the *The Bon Appétit Cookbook*. It's just really good meatloaf. I think the tomatoes add moisture to the mix, as well as the milk and eggs. After coming across several different mash combinations, this one caught my eye. I've adjusted it to my taste as the years have gone by. Try the entire combination for a casual supper, and you'll be very pleased.

turkey meatloaf

1 large onion, chopped
1½ tablespoons extra-virgin olive oil
3 stalks celery, chopped
1½ pounds ground turkey
1½ cups fresh bread crumbs from soft bread
⅔ cup drained and chopped oil-packed sun-dried tomatoes
½ cup milk
2 eggs
1 teaspoon fresh chopped sage leaves
1 teaspoon fresh chopped oregano leaves
Kosher salt and freshly ground black pepper, to taste
Ketchup, as needed

1. Grease a 9" x 5" x 3" loaf pan. Preheat oven to 375 degrees.

2. In a pan over medium heat, saute the onion in the oil for 5 minutes (do not brown).

3. Add the celery and saute until tender (about 10 minutes). Transfer the mixture to a large bowl and allow it to cool.

4. Add all of the remaining ingredients except the ketchup to the vegetables in the bowl; mix thoroughly. Saute a small sample of the mixture to taste and correct for seasoning.

5. Transfer the raw mixture to the prepared loaf pan. Bake in the 375-degree oven for about 1 hour. Brush the top with ketchup to give it a nice coating; continue to bake until the internal temperature reaches 160 degrees. Remove it from the oven and allow it to cool 5 minutes; remove from the pan. Cut into 12 slices (giving each person 2 slices).

leeks

1 bunch leeks
6 tablespoons unsalted butter
¼ cup white wine
½ cup heavy cream
Kosher salt and freshly ground black pepper, to taste

1. Trim the roots and most, but not all, of the green leaves from the leeks. Split them down the center and soak in water, washing away any sand. Remove from the water and pat dry. Chop the leeks into half moons.

2. In a large saute pan, melt the butter. When it begins to bubble, add the leeks and slowly cook them; don't let them brown.

3. Deglaze the pan with the white wine and reduce the liquid until the pan is dry. Add the heavy cream and season with salt and pepper, to taste.

4. When the leeks are tender, set the pan aside to cool.

mash

3 pounds Idaho potatoes, peeled and cut into chunks
Kosher salt, to taste
¼ pound unsalted butter, cubed
Freshly ground black pepper, to taste
1 cup warm milk

1. Place the potatoes in a pot with cold salted water (to cover). Bring to a boil over high heat and then reduce to a simmer.

2. Preheat oven to 400 degrees.

3. Cook the potatoes until they are fork tender. Drain them and then spread them out on a sheet pan; place in the 400-degree oven for a few minutes to dry out.

4. Mash the potatoes with a potato masher, adding the butter and seasoning with salt and pepper, to taste.

5. Add the milk, as needed, until you reach the desired consistency (you may not need all of it).

6. Add the leeks and combine well. Keep warm or rewarm in the microwave.

green beans

½ teaspoon kosher salt, plus more to taste
1½ pounds green beans
Unsalted butter, as needed
Extra-virgin olive oil, as needed
Freshly ground black pepper, to taste

1. Bring a pot of water to a boil and add the salt. Drop in the beans and cook them just until tender (3-4 minutes). Drain and immediately plunge them into ice water to stop the cooking process. Drain again and pat dry.

2. Reheat in a saute pan with a little butter and olive oil. Season with salt and pepper, to taste.

assembly

1. Reheat the meatloaf in a warm oven with a little water to prevent the loaf from drying.

2. In the center of each of 6 plates, spoon a dollop of the leek/potato mash. Angle 2 slices of the turkey meatloaf on the mash. Position the green beans to the left of the center.

Serves 6

Marinated lamb T-bones with Himalayan red rice and sauteed broccoli rabe

This lamb marinade is one I've been using for years, with a little honey for sweetness and lavender from my garden. I use the flowers in summer and the chopped stems other times. If you can get your hands on this rice, definitely try it; otherwise, brown rice works well. The broccoli rabe recipe was inspired from the Zuni Café. I wanted to try an alternative way to present this vegetable, and this is a different technique.

marinated lamb

½ cup extra-virgin olive oil
1 cup white wine
1 tablespoon freshly ground black pepper
1 tablespoon honey
2 tablespoons fresh lavender flowers
1 tablespoon soy sauce
8 lamb T-bones

1. In a small bowl, combine all of the ingredients except the lamb. Place the T-bones in a roomy dish and pour the marinade over them. Allow them to marinate in the refrigerator for at least 8 hours or overnight.

2. Preheat grill. Grill the T-bones over a medium-high heat for about 5 minutes per side or until browned to desired doneness. Let rest.

Himalayan red rice

1 cup red rice (or brown rice)
2 stalks celery, diced
½ cup pecan halves
4 green onions, chopped
Extra-virgin olive oil, as needed
Kosher salt and freshly ground black pepper, to taste
1 cup vegetable stock

1. Cook the rice according to package directions and allow it to cool.

2. Preheat oven to 400 degrees.

3. While the rice is cooking, bring a separate pot of water to a boil over high heat. Drop the celery into the boiling water to blanch (about 3 minutes). Drain and then refresh under cold running water; drain well.

4. Place the pecans on a sheet tray. Toast the nuts in the 400-degree oven until golden. Check after 3 minutes and watch carefully until lightly toasted. Remove from the oven, allow to cool and then chop.

3. Toss the cooled rice with the celery, pecans and onions.

4. Drizzle in the olive oil and season, to taste, with salt and pepper. Reheat as needed in a saute pan with vegetable stock.

grilled broccoli rabe

About 12 ounces broccoli rabe, trimmed
3-4 tablespoons extra-virgin olive oil
About 1 tablespoon water
Kosher salt, to taste

1. Split any stalks of broccoli rabe that are more than ½-inch thick. Toss the rabe as you would a salad with the olive oil, water and salt, to taste. Leave to soften 5-10 minutes at room temperature.

2. Preheat grill to high heat.

3. Arrange the broccoli on the hot grill and cook for about 1½ minutes per side, allowing the leaves and flowerets to char slightly as the water steams the thicker stems to tenderness. Slide the rabe into a deep roasting pan and keep until needed. (Don't stack the rabe, or you will compromise its pleasant papery-fleshy texture.) Serve at room temperature.

assembly

1. Place the rice in the center of each of 4 plates. Wrap the rabe around the rice (nest style). Place 2 T-bones on each dish. (An alternative presentation appears in the photo on page 22.)

Serves 4

Filet of beef with spring fava beans and radishes and French feta cheese

A filet could just sit on the plate alone, but I always think the starch/vegetable brings out the best in the dish. A few years ago in *Bon Appétit*, there was a salad with fava beans and feta cheese. I embellished the dish with additional items and made it my own. This vegetable toss goes well with lots of main-course items.

dressing

3 tablespoons apple cider vinegar
2 teaspoons Dijon mustard
¼ cup extra-virgin olive oil
Kosher salt and freshly ground black pepper, to taste

1. Whisk together the vinegar and mustard in a small bowl. Gradually whisk in the olive oil and season with salt and pepper, to taste.
2. Cover and chill in the refrigerator.

vegetable toss

2 cups fresh fava beans or edamame
Kosher salt, to taste
1 pound Yukon gold potatoes
2 tablespoons vegetable oil
Freshly ground black pepper, to taste
10 medium-size radishes, very thinly sliced
1 bunch green onions, cut on the diagonal
¼ cup chopped fresh herbs (such as tarragon, basil, thyme and parsley)

1. Cook the fava beans in a large pot of boiling salted water until tender (about 2 minutes).
2. Transfer the beans to a bowl of ice water to cool. Drain and then peel them, patting the beans dry with paper towels.
3. Place the potatoes in a 4-quart saucepan with cold water and a generous amount of salt. Bring to a boil over high heat and then lower heat; simmer the potatoes until they are just tender, and the edges are starting to soften. Drain and, when cool, slice them.
4. In a large saute pan, heat the vegetable oil over medium heat. Brown the sliced potatoes until golden. Season with salt and pepper, to taste. Remove from the pan and place in a large bowl.
5. To the bowl, add the radishes, onions, herbs and dressing; toss well. Season with salt and pepper, to taste.

filet of beef

1-1½ pounds beef tenderloin, trimmed of fat and silver skin, portioned into 4 filets (4-6 ounces each)
Kosher salt and freshly ground black pepper, to taste
1 tablespoon unsalted butter
1 tablespoon vegetable oil

1. Preheat oven to 400 degrees. Season the filets with salt and pepper.
2. Heat a large skillet with an oven-safe handle over high heat. When the skillet is smoking, add the butter and vegetable oil, and then the filets. Sear on both sides (about 3 minutes on each side).
3. Transfer to the 400-degree oven and cook about 7-10 more minutes for medium-rare to well done. Check with an instant-read thermometer after 5 minutes. Remove when you have reached your desired doneness (see Internal Temperatures for Cooking Meat on page 7). Let rest for 3 minutes.
4. Slice each portion on an angle into 3 thick slices.

assembly

⅓-½ cup small-dice feta cheese
Extra-virgin olive oil, to finish

1. Divide the vegetable toss among 4 plates and top with the filet (3 slices each).
2. Garnish with feta cheese and drizzle with a little olive oil to finish the plate.

Serves 4

"These sai

Strawberry and mango sable

There are times when I want strawberries, but not as a shortcake dessert. Here is a nice, easy alternative. This sable recipe is from Balleymaloe Cookery School in Ireland, which I attended for a three-month period back in the mid-'90s. These sable biscuits could be paired with other fruits and can be frozen.

biscuits

6 ounces all-purpose flour *
⅔ cup confectioners' sugar
1 pinch salt
2½ tablespoons unsalted butter
1 egg yolk

1. Sieve the flour and sugar into a bowl and add a tiny pinch of salt.

2. Rub in the butter and the yolk, pressing the mixture together. (Alternatively, make the dough in a food processor, stopping the machine just as soon as the mixture comes together.) Wrap the dough in plastic wrap and let rest for 30 minutes in the refrigerator.

3. Preheat oven to 350 degrees.

4. On a lightly floured surface, roll out the pastry into an ⅛-inch-thick sheet. Stamp out 12 circles with a 3½-inch fluted pastry cutter.

5. Place the circles onto a baking sheet lined with parchment paper. Bake in the 350-degree oven about 15-20 minutes. They will be pale golden in color when they are done. Remove from the oven.

strawberry and mango mixture

½ pound strawberries, cleaned, hulled and sliced
1 mango, peeled, seeded and diced
1 tablespoon granulated sugar, plus more to taste

1. Combine all of the ingredients and let macerate. Adjust flavor as needed with more sugar.

assembly

10 ounces whipping cream
6 mint leaves, to garnish (optional)

1. Whip the cream until soft peaks form.

2. Place 1 biscuit on each serving plate and top with a little whipped cream and then the strawberry and mango mixture. Top with another biscuit and a dollop of cream. Garnish with a mint leaf, if desired. Drizzle a little juice on each plate, surrounding the biscuits. (An alternative presentation appears in the photo on page 26.)

Serves 6

*Use a scale to accurately measure the flour.

summer

Farmers markets and produce stands are in full swing, and issues of availability that we struggle with throughout the rest of the year have passed.

Peppery radishes, sweet raspberries and juicy peaches are ready to enjoy, and local chickens and eggs are easier to find. During the summer months, keep the house cooler and time spent in the kitchen to a minimum by using quick-cook methods and grilling often. From mid-June through September, there is so much bursting forth in fields and farms — so just live it up.

Peach, almond, Parmesan and mixed leaf salad tossed in champagne-peach dressing

This peach dressing is perfect on summer leaves. I adapted the recipe several years ago from a cooking magazine. I have added duck to this salad as well, which would be a wonderful summer dinner item. The dressing makes enough for about eight salads, so store the remaining vinaigrette in the refrigerator for another time.

peach vinaigrette

3 peaches, skin on, pitted
¼ cup champagne vinegar
¾ cup oil (half extra-virgin olive and half vegetable oil)
Kosher salt and freshly ground pepper, to taste
Sugar, to taste

1. Puree the peaches in a blender or food processor.
2. Pour 1½ cups of the peach puree into a mixing bowl. Whisk in the vinegar and then the oils until an emulsion has been reached.
3. Season with salt and pepper, and sugar, to taste.

salad

¼ cup sliced almonds
4 handfuls mixed leaves
½ red onion, julienned
2 ripe peaches, skin on, sliced
2 ripe apricots, skin on, sliced
Parmesan cheese, shaved (using a vegetable peeler), to garnish

It makes enough for about eight salads."

1. Preheat oven to 400 degrees. Place the almonds on a small sheet tray. Toast the nuts in the 400-degree oven until golden. Check after 3 minutes and watch carefully until lightly toasted. Remove from the oven and allow to cool.

2. Toss the leaves and onion in enough dressing to coat well and then divide among 4 plates. Toss the peaches and apricots in more of the dressing and place on the plates. Garnish with the toasted almonds and shaved Parmesan.

Serves 4

Indiana watermelon with prosciutto de Parma and Gorgonzola

This is a beautiful summer combination, similar to cantaloupe with prosciutto, but with a twist. Look for local watermelon in August, when farmers markets are brimming with produce at its peak.

½ watermelon, meat seeded and cut into chunks
8 thin slices prosciutto de Parma ham
¾ cup crumbled Gorgonzola
8-10 mint leaves, chiffonade (cut into ribbon-like strips)
Extra-virgin olive oil, to taste
Freshly ground black pepper, to taste

1. On each of 4 cold plates, place several chunks of the watermelon.

2. For each serving, layer 2 ham slices over the melon. Top with crumbles of cheese and slices of mint.

3. Drizzle with olive oil and a grind of black pepper, to taste.

Serves 4

Succotash atop a zucchini pancake and sliced tomatoes

This is my version of succotash combined from several recipes I've reviewed. The zucchini pancake is adapted from a recipe by Italian cookbook author Giuliano Bugialli. This is a great summertime vegetarian combination with sliced tomatoes, the tender pancakes and a topping of succotash. Delicious!

corn stock

8 ears corn
1 onion, chopped
1 carrot, chopped
1 bay leaf

1. Shuck and cut the kernels from the ears of corn, reserving the cobs and kernels (for use in the corn succotash below).

2. Into a stockpot, place the cobs, onion, carrot and bay leaf. Cover the vegetables with cold water and place on a burner over high heat. Bring to a boil and then simmer for about 30 minutes.

3. Strain, and you have corn stock. (Use as a soup base and in the corn succotash below.)

corn succotash

2 tablespoons extra-virgin olive oil, plus more as needed
1 tablespoon unsalted butter
¾ cup minced scallions (white and light green parts only)
1 zucchini, diced
1 yellow bell pepper, diced
1 red bell pepper, diced
1½ cups fresh corn kernels (or frozen, thawed)
¾ cup corn stock (recipe above)
¼ cup heavy whipping cream
Kosher salt and freshly ground black pepper, to taste

1. Heat the 2 tablespoons olive oil and butter in a large skillet over medium-high heat. Add the scallions and cook gently for 1 minute, until slightly soft.

2. Add the zucchini, peppers and corn kernels and cook for 3 minutes, stirring frequently.

3. Stir in the corn stock and cream; simmer until the liquid is reduced to a thick, creamy consistency (2-3 minutes). Season with salt and pepper, to taste. (Allow it to cool while you make the zucchini pancakes. You can reheat with a touch of cream right before serving.)

zucchini pancakes*

1 pound zucchini, rinsed
Zest of 1 lemon with thick skin
10 sprigs Italian parsley, leaves only, chopped
1 small clove garlic, chopped
Kosher salt and freshly ground black pepper, to taste
2 large eggs
½ cup flour
About 1 cup vegetable oil

1. Coarsely grate the zucchini into a bowl. Add the lemon zest, parsley and garlic and mix well; season with salt and pepper, to taste.

2. Add the eggs and mix well.

3. Add the flour, a little at a time, constantly mixing with a wooden spoon.

4. Have a sheet tray lined with paper towels at the ready. Heat about 2 tablespoons of the vegetable oil in a large skillet over medium heat. Scoop up about ¼ cup of the mixture and gently drop into the skillet to form a pancake. (You can make 3-4 at a time.) When they are lightly golden on the bottom, use a spatula to turn them over; when they are lightly golden on both sides, transfer to the sheet tray, being sure they are cooked through. Before adding more mixture to the skillet, pour in more oil if necessary. Mix the pancake batter after each batch.

5. Sprinkle the pancakes with salt and serve hot.

assembly

1 large tomato, cut into 4 slices
Kosher salt and freshly ground black pepper, to taste
Chopped chives, to garnish

1. On each of 4 plates, place 2 warm zucchini pancakes and 1 slice tomato; season the tomato with salt and pepper, to taste.

2. Top with a heaping portion of corn succotash and garnish with chopped chives. (An alternative presentation incorporating 2 tomato slices and eliminating the chopped chives appears on page 34.)

Serves 4

*This recipe can be prepared in advance, grating the zucchini and placing it in a colander until needed. In a different bowl, prepare the batter and combine the zucchini and batter when you're ready to cook the pancakes.

Roasted red pepper stuffed with green and wax beans, feta cheese and kalamata olives

When I was working at the Yorke Arms in North Yorkshire, England, this was a popular vegetarian dish on the menu. It has lots of flavor and beautiful colors.

red wine vinaigrette

⅓ cup red wine vinegar
1 teaspoon sugar, or to taste
Kosher salt and freshly ground black pepper, to taste
1 tablespoon Dijon mustard
⅔ cup oil (half extra-virgin olive and half vegetable oil)

1. Whisk together all of the ingredients except oils.
2. Slowly drizzle in the oils, whisking constantly, to emulsify.

stuffed pepper

4 red bell peppers
Extra-virgin olive oil, as needed
½ teaspoon kosher salt, plus more as needed, to taste
½ pound green beans or wax beans (or a combination of both), trimmed
¼ pound small red-skinned potatoes
½ red onion, julienned
Freshly ground black pepper, to taste
16 kalamata olives, pitted and roughly chopped
4 ounces feta cheese, diced *
1 handful fresh basil chiffonade (cut into ribbon-like strips)

1. Preheat oven to 400 degrees.
2. Rub the peppers with a little olive oil and place them on a sheet pan. Roast in the 400-degree oven 15-25 minutes, turning as they brown and blister. Transfer to a large bowl and cover with plastic wrap to let the peppers steam. (Keep the oven on.) Let the peppers cool.
3. When the peppers are cool, gently peel them, removing the seeds and stems, but keeping the shell of pepper intact as much as possible.
4. Bring a small pot of water to a boil and add ½ teaspoon salt. Drop in the beans and cook them 3-4 minutes, just until tender. Drain and immediately plunge them into ice water to stop the cooking process. Drain again and pat dry.
5. Place the potatoes in a 4-quart pot and cover with cold water; salt the water liberally. With the pot uncovered, bring the water to a boil and cook the potatoes until just tender with softened edges. Drain, cool and then cut into quarters.
6. Toss the onion with 1 tablespoon olive oil, and salt and pepper, to taste. Spread the onion evenly on a sheet pan and roast in the 400-degree oven for about 8 minutes, checking them often and turning them to prevent the edges from burning. Remove from the oven and allow to cool.
7. In a large mixing bowl, combine the beans, potatoes, onion, olives, feta cheese and basil; toss gently. Drizzle with the red wine vinaigrette and season with salt and pepper, to taste.

assembly

1. On each of 4 separate plates, place a roasted pepper skin side down and opened. Place a handful of salad in the pepper and then close the pepper over part of the salad to make it look attractive. Drizzle with additional vinaigrette on the salad and plate.

Serves 4

*French feta cheese is milder than the variety usually found in the grocery store. Use it if you can find it.

Vegetable Wellington with Swiss chard

I've made several types of Wellingtons through the years. We're all familiar with beef or salmon wrapped in light pastry, but I wanted a vegetarian version. The duxelles is a combination from a beef Wellington I've done in the past.

mushroom duxelles

2 cups mushrooms (such as oyster and crimini), cleaned and trimmed if necessary
2 cups roughly chopped green onions
1½ cups white wine
Kosher salt and freshly ground black pepper, to taste

1. Process the mushrooms and onions in a food processor until finely chopped and then scrape into a saucepan.
2. Cover the vegetables with white wine. Reduce over medium-high heat until the mixture is dry. (Be careful not to burn it.) Season with salt and pepper, to taste. Remove from heat.

vegetables

Kosher salt, to taste
½ pound green beans, topped and tailed
½ green cabbage, quartered, cored and thinly sliced
1 medium-size zucchini, cut into ½-inch slices
1 yellow squash, cut into ½-inch slices
2 tablespoons extra-virgin olive oil
Freshly ground black pepper, to taste
1 large red tomato, cut into 4 thick slices

1. Bring a pot of salted water to a boil. Drop in the beans and cook them 3-5 minutes, just until tender. Scoop out the beans and immediately plunge them into ice water to stop the cooking process. Drain again and pat dry; set aside.
2. In the same boiling salted water, add the cabbage and blanch for 2-3 minutes, just until tender. Drain, refresh in ice water and drain again; set aside.
3. Toss the zucchini and yellow squash in the olive oil; season with salt and pepper, to taste. Heat a grill pan and grill the vegetables on both sides until just tender but not too soft. Set aside.
4. Be sure all the vegetables, including the tomato slices, are seasoned with salt and pepper, to taste, and ready to use.

Wellingtons

1 egg
1 tablespoon water
1 sheet premade puff pastry (4 servings per sheet), thawed

All-purpose flour, as needed
Fresh chopped herbs (such as basil and parsley), to taste

1. Whisk together the egg and water. Line a sheet pan with parchment paper. Preheat oven to 425 degrees.
2. Unfold the pastry on a lightly floured surface. Cut into 4 quarters. Roll out each quarter into about a 7-inch square.
3. Spread about 2 tablespoons mushroom duxelles onto the center of each square and then top with about 8-10 beans (lined up symmetrically). Layer 2 slices zucchini and then two slices yellow squash; sprinkle with herbs. Top with 1 tomato slice and add more herbs.
4. Brush the edges of the pastry with the egg wash. Fold over two opposing sides and then the other two sides, sealing the seams.
5. Carefully turn over each completed Wellington onto the parchment paper. Brush each with the egg wash. Place in the refrigerator for about 15 minutes to set the pastry.
6. Bake in the 425-degree oven until golden (15-20 minutes), checking them periodically to be sure they do not over brown.

Swiss chard

1½ pounds Swiss chard, washed well and drained
1 tablespoon vegetable oil
1 tablespoon unsalted butter
Kosher salt and freshly ground black pepper, to taste
2 tablespoons sherry vinegar

1. Cut the stems and thick center ribs from the Swiss chard leaves. Discard the ribs, coarsely chop the stems and cut the leaves into chiffonade (ribbon-like strips).
2. In a large saute pan over medium-high heat, add the oil and butter and then the stems, sauteing for a few minutes. Add the leaves and saute until wilted; season with salt and pepper, to taste.
3. Add the vinegar and toss well.

assembly

1. On 4 dinner plates, place a portion of seasoned Swiss chard, being sure to shake off any excess liquid.
2. Place a Wellington to the side of the leaves and serve.

Serves 4

Seared scallops with summer fingerlings and beans and yellow tomato gazpacho

During the summer, there are so many tomatoes available that it's the perfect time to make gazpacho. You could use red tomatoes, but this is a nice change with yellow tomatoes. The gazpacho is based on a recipe we used when working with Volker Rudolph at the Canterbury Hotel downtown. There is, of course, a vegetable toss to balance out the dish with a starch. If runner beans aren't available, use green beans. The scallops only take moments to pan-sear. This presents perfectly as a summer dinner party entree if you serve five scallops per person.

yellow tomato gazpacho

3 yellow tomatoes, peeled * and seeded †
3 bell peppers (1 each, red, green and yellow), stems,
**   seeds and pith removed; roughly chopped**
½ red onion, roughly chopped
2 cloves garlic
1 cucumber, peeled, seeded and roughly chopped
2 cups vegetable stock
1 tablespoon chopped parsley
⅓ cup extra-virgin olive oil
Kosher salt and freshly ground black pepper, to taste

1. In a food processor, puree all of the vegetables, adding stock as needed to reach your desired soup consistency. Transfer each batch of pureed ingredients to a large bowl.
2. Whisk in the parsley, olive oil, and salt and pepper, to taste. Adjust the seasonings or broth amount as needed and refrigerate until ready to serve.

vegetable toss

1 pound fingerling potatoes, halved
Kosher salt, to taste
1 pound runner beans, cut on an angle
Butter, as needed
Extra-virgin olive oil, as needed
Freshly ground black pepper, to taste
½ cup chopped Italian flat-leaf parsley

1. Place the potatoes in a 4-quart pot and cover with cold water; liberally salt the water. Bring to a boil and cook until they are just tender, and the edges are starting to soften. Drain and then cool on a sheet pan; cut into quarters.
2. Bring a separate pot of salted water to a boil over high heat. Drop in the beans and cook until al dente (about 3-5 minutes, check to your own desired doneness). Drain immediately and plunge in ice water to stop the cooking process. Drain again and pat dry.

3. In a large skillet over medium heat, place a dollop of butter and a dash of olive oil and heat. Toss in the fingerlings and cook until golden; add the beans and cook through. Season with salt and pepper, to taste. Add a handful of chopped parsley to finish and toss.

seared scallops

Kosher salt and freshly ground black pepper, to taste
1-1½ pounds scallops (5 scallops per person for
**   entree size)**
Vegetable oil, as needed

1. Lightly salt and pepper the scallops.
2. Heat a large saute pan over high heat with oil, as needed. When the oil is sizzling hot, gingerly place the scallops in the pan. Sear on one side until browned (this will not take long). When they can be pulled away nicely, turn them and finish the cooking process on the other side until done. Remove from the pan.

assembly

1. In the center of each of 4 wide soup bowls, place a mound of the vegetable toss. Ladle the yellow tomato gazpacho around the vegetables. Place 5 seared scallops on top of the vegetables and serve. (As an alternative presentation, serve 1 scallop per person as a first course, as shown in the photo on page 40.)

Serves 4

*To skin tomatoes, bring a large pot of water to a boil; have ready a bowl of ice water and a metal strainer for scooping the tomatoes from the pot. Core the tomatoes and place an "X" on the bottom of each. Drop 2-3 tomatoes in the boiling water, count to 10 and remove them to the ice water. The skin should be a little loose and peel in the ice water. Remove and place on kitchen towels.

†To seed tomatoes, slice them in half across the equator. Set a strainer over a bowl to catch the juice as you remove the seeds. The juice can be added back with the tomato pulp. Gently squeeze the tomatoes, using your fingers to loosen the seeds.

Smoked trout with red onion, cucumber and tomato salad

Each week I come up with several new menu items, which can be difficult at times. But during the summer, when tomatoes, cucumbers and radishes are abundant, this is the ideal salad for utilizing all that good produce. I wanted to use all of these fresh ingredients and top it with smoked trout, and here is the result. It's really a basic dressing and seasonal vegetables.

dressing

1 tablespoon granulated sugar
1 teaspoon salt
½ teaspoon freshly ground black pepper
1 heaping teaspoon Dijon mustard
2 tablespoons cider vinegar
¼ cup extra-virgin olive oil

1. In a small bowl, whisk together all of the ingredients except the oil.
2. Slowly pour in the oil, whisking constantly until well blended. Set aside.

salad and trout

1 large red onion, cut into ½-inch dice
Kosher salt, to taste
8 ounces smoked trout
4 seedless cucumbers, peeled and sliced ⅓-inch thick
3 large tomatoes, cored and cut into ½-inch dice
6 large meaty radishes, thinly sliced
1 tablespoon roughly chopped parsley
Freshly ground black pepper, to taste

1. Soak the red onion in a small bowl of salted ice water for 20 minutes, and then drain well. (This will make the onion milder and more digestible.)
2. Prep the trout by skinning it and removing the gray area. Roughly crumble the fish. Keep separate.
3. Toss the vegetables and parsley in the dressing (just enough to coat). Season with salt and pepper, to taste.
4. On each of 4 chilled plates, place the vegetable-parsley toss in the center. Top with the crumbled trout.

Serves 4

"The lentil salad is a very simple combination, bu

Broiled Alaskan halibut on a lentil salad with sliced tomatoes and feta

In this dish, Alaskan halibut is paired with lentils, sliced Indiana tomatoes, olives and feta cheese. A very simple combination, but loaded with flavor, the lentil salad recipe is an adaptation from a recipe I found on the Internet.

broiled halibut

½ cup vegetable oil
1½ pounds halibut filets, skinless, boneless and cut into 4 6-ounce portions (ask your fishmonger to prepare the halibut)
Kosher salt and freshly ground black pepper, to taste

1. Preheat broiler. Line a heavy baking sheet with foil and coat the foil with cooking spray.

2. Pour the oil onto a small tray and lay the halibut in it to lightly coat. Season the top of the fish with salt and the bottom of the fish with salt and pepper, to taste.

3. Place the halibut on the prepared baking sheet and place under the broiler. Broil 3-4 inches from the flame until the ends start to become golden (6-9 minutes). Check the fish frequently to be sure it is not overcooking. Remove from heat and set aside.

Turkish lentil salad

1 cup dried French green lentils
7 tablespoons extra-virgin olive oil, plus more to taste
1½ tablespoons lemon juice, plus more to taste
Kosher salt and freshly ground black pepper, to taste
½ onion, finely chopped
1 clove garlic, minced
1 teaspoon cumin
2 tablespoons chopped mint
2 tablespoons chopped parsley

1. Put the lentils in a saucepan and cover with cold water. Bring to a boil, and then reduce heat to low and simmer gently until they are tender but not falling apart. (The timing will depend upon the age of the lentils, so you will want to test them from time to time, starting at 20 minutes. Some can take as long as 40 minutes, others may be tender in 25 minutes.)

2. Drain the lentils and transfer to a bowl. While they are still warm, dress with 4 tablespoons of the olive oil and all of the lemon juice; sprinkle with salt and pepper, to taste.

3. Heat the remaining 3 tablespoons olive oil in a saute pan over medium heat. Add the onion and cook until tender.

4. Add the garlic and cumin and cook 1-2 minutes longer. Remove from heat and let cool; add to the lentils and toss to combine. Dress the salad with additional lemon juice and oil, and salt and pepper, to taste. Stir in the herbs. Serve at room temperature or slightly chilled.

assembly

2 ripe tomatoes, cut into 8 slices
4 ounces crumbled French (or Greek) feta cheese, to garnish
Kosher salt, to taste
½ cup parsley chiffonade (cut into ribbon-like strips)
12 kalamata olives, pitted, to garnish

1. Set up 4 dinner plates. On each, place 2 slices tomato; place a spoonful of Turkish lentil salad over 1 of the slices. Top the other slice with feta cheese, salt, to taste, and parsley. Angle a broiled halibut filet on the salad. Garnish with 3 olives. (An alternative presentation appears in the photo on page 44.)

Serves 4

"Panzanella is an Italian bread salad that

Prosciutto-wrapped Alaskan halibut on panzanella

Panzanella is an Italian bread salad that is perfect in the summertime when tomatoes and cucumbers are at their peak. This is an adapted recipe from one of my Italian cookbooks, to which I added a few items. The halibut is also at its best in summer, and when wrapped with prosciutto, it looks great. Lots of color in this dish. The dressing has plenty of flavor with the combination of red wine and balsamic vinegars.

prosciutto-wrapped halibut

2 6-ounce skinless, boneless halibut filets
2 very thin slices prosciutto
Vegetable oil, as needed
Kosher salt and freshly ground black pepper, to taste

1. Preheat oven to 400 degrees.
2. Wrap the prosciutto all the way around the halibut. Oil and lightly season it with salt and pepper.
3. Transfer to a baking dish and roast in the 400-degree oven until the fish is cooked through (about 12-15 minutes). If you think your prosciutto should be crisper, turn on your broiler and pass the ham under it for a few seconds, watching it carefully, and remove.

basic vinaigrette

3 tablespoons red wine vinegar
1 tablespoon balsamic vinegar
1 teaspoon Dijon mustard
Kosher salt and freshly ground black pepper, to taste
1 clove garlic, minced
1 cup oil (half extra-virgin olive and half vegetable oil)

1. Whisk together all of the basic vinaigrette ingredients except oils until combined.
2. Whisking constantly, slowly pour in the oils to emulsify. You can also add more minced garlic, to taste. (This will keep in the refrigerator for 2 weeks.)

panzanella (Italian bread salad)

2 cups 1-inch-square bread cubes (Asiago or another cheese bread is delicious, trimmed of any hard crusts)
Extra-virgin olive oil, as needed
1 cup diced tomato
1 cup diced cucumber (peeled and seeded if necessary)
Finely chopped red onion, to taste
2 tablespoons fresh basil chiffonade (cut into ribbon-like strips), plus more to taste
2 tablespoons chopped parsley
1 cup sliced celery
½ cup halved mixed olives

1. Preheat oven to 400 degrees.
2. Toss the bread cubes in a little olive oil; spread them out on a sheet pan and toast in the 400-degree oven until golden.
3. In a large bowl, toss the bread with 2 tablespoons of the basic vinaigrette and let stand about 30 minutes.
4. Add the remaining panzanella ingredients. Pour in enough dressing to coat and quickly toss together. Garnish with a little more basil chiffonade, if necessary.

assembly

Extra-virgin olive oil, to taste

1. Place the panzanella on a plate and top with the halibut. Drizzle with a little olive oil, to taste.

Serves 2

"The salad is an alternative to classic potato sala

Broiled filet of salmon resting on a bed of Sicilian potato/tomato salad

This salmon can either be grilled or broiled. The salad is an alternative to classic potato salad, utilizing tomatoes and olives with fresh oregano from your garden.

salmon (grill and broil methods)

4 6-ounce salmon filets
Vegetable oil, as needed
Kosher salt and freshly ground black pepper, to taste

grill method

1. Prepare the grill, preheating to medium-high heat. Lightly brush the salmon with oil; sprinkle with salt and pepper, to taste.

2. Grill the fish, skin side up, until just opaque in the center (about 5 minutes per side). Turn and finish grilling. Remove and let rest.

broil method

1. Preheat broiler. Arrange the salmon, skin side down, on a foil-lined broiler pan. Brush with vegetable oil and season with salt and pepper, to taste.

2. Broil without turning until just opaque in the center (about 7-9 minutes).

Sicilian potato/tomato salad

1½ pounds red new potatoes (or fingerlings), scrubbed
Kosher salt, to taste
**4 ripe tomatoes (1 pound), sliced ⅜-inch thick and
  then chopped**
1 small red onion, thinly sliced
½ cup kalamata olives, pitted
1 tablespoon capers, rinsed
½ cup extra-virgin olive oil
2 teaspoons dried or freshly chopped oregano

1. Place the potatoes in a 4-quart saucepan with enough cold water to cover well and a generous amount of salt. Bring to a boil over high heat and then lower heat to simmer the potatoes until they are just tender, and the edges are starting to soften. Drain and, when cool, cut into bite-size pieces.

2. In a large bowl, combine the potatoes, tomatoes, onion, olives and capers. Pour the olive oil over it all and sprinkle with oregano and salt, to taste. Gingerly turn the salad to coat.

assembly

1. Divide the salad among 4 plates and top with the salmon.

Serves 4

Indiana beefsteak tomato stuffed with Cobb salad

A chef who worked with me for the first few years at R bistro suggested that we try a Cobb salad-stuffed tomato. I thought of all the ingredients I like in a Cobb and came up with our version. The dressing with paprika, dried mustard and seasoned salt is a recipe I've been using for about 25 years. It came out of a church cookbook from Windber, Pennsylvania. We sometimes say, "It's the best dressing ever!" It goes well with a green salad or a vegetable toss.

beefsteak tomatoes

4 large beefsteak tomatoes, tops removed

1. Use a melon baller to remove the pulp and seeds from the tomatoes, reserving the pulp and roughly chopping it. Turn the hollowed-out tomatoes upside down on paper towels to drain.

poached chicken breasts

3 cups cold water
1 cup dry white wine
½ carrot, sliced
½ onion, sliced
2 cloves garlic, sliced
1 tablespoon salt
Few sprigs parsley
2 sprigs thyme
2 bay leaves
1½ pounds boneless, skinless chicken breasts (about 4 breast halves)

1. Prepare a simple court bouillon by combining all of the poached chicken breasts ingredients except the chicken in a deep skillet or Dutch oven. (These ingredients can be modified with different herbs, vinegar in place of wine, and other vegetables such as chopped tomatoes and fennel.) Bring to a boil and then reduce heat, allowing the liquid to simmer for about 15 minutes.

2. Add the chicken to the poaching liquid and reduce heat; cover and slowly cook until the breasts reach 160 degrees (about 20 minutes). Remove from heat and, when they're cool enough to handle, chop into ½-inch dice.

dressing

½ cup sugar
1 teaspoon paprika
1 teaspoon dried mustard
1 teaspoon seasoned salt (such as Lawry's Seasoned Salt)
½ medium-size onion, finely grated
1 cup salad oil (such as canola or grapeseed)
¼ cup red wine vinegar

1. In the bowl of a stand-up mixer, or using a hand-held mixer and a bowl, blend the sugar, paprika, dried mustard and seasoned salt.

2. Whisk the finely grated onion into the dry ingredients and mix until the sugar is dissolved.

3. At a slow speed on the mixer, begin to add the salad oil, a little at a time. Mix well. Add a portion of the vinegar and mix well. Continue until all of the oil and vinegar have been added. Be sure to finish with the vinegar.

4. Beat at high speed until it has reached the degree of thickness you want. Set aside.

filling

½ pound bacon, cut into ½-inch pieces, cooked until crisp
4 eggs, hard-boiled and chopped
2 avocados, chopped
1 cup corn (fresh or frozen)
4 ounces goat cheese, crumbled
Fresh chopped oregano, to taste
½ cup pine nuts, toasted
Reserved chopped tomato pulp
Kosher salt and freshly ground black pepper, to taste

1. Prep all of the filling ingredients and have them nearby.

(recipe continued on page 52)

(Indiana beefsteak tomato stuffed with Cobb salad, continued from page 51)

red wine vinaigrette

⅓ cup extra-virgin olive oil
⅔ cup vegetable oil
4 tablespoons red wine vinegar
1 teaspoon Dijon mustard
Kosher salt and freshly ground black pepper, to taste
1 pinch sugar, or to taste

1. Whisk all of the ingredients together or process in a blender until combined. Adjust with any of the ingredients to suit your taste.

assembly

1 head romaine lettuce, chopped
Chopped parsley, to garnish

1. In a large bowl, combine all of the filling items with the chopped chicken. Add the first dressing (just enough to coat) and gently toss.

2. In a separate bowl, toss the chopped romaine with the red wine vinaigrette (just enough to coat) and divide equally among 4 cold plates.*

3. Spoon the filling into each of the beefsteak tomatoes and let a little spill out the sides. Place on top of the leaves and drizzle with a little extra dressing. Garnish with chopped parsley. (An alternative presentation appears in the photo on page 50.)

Serves 4

*Always dress leaves lightly and gently toss. Do not place dry leaves on a plate and pour dressing on top. Leaves need to be tossed.

Grilled chicken breast with watermelon and jicama salad in a bowl of watermelon soup

One of my interns from the Ivy Tech Community College of Indiana culinary program gave me this watermelon soup recipe several years ago. I kept thinking about how to adapt it as a main course here at the restaurant and held onto it for a few seasons. Then I decided to create a radish salad as a base, pour the soup around the salad and top it with a grilled boneless chicken breast. I think it's a perfectly fresh, light summer dinner item.

watermelon and jicama salad

10 radishes, thinly sliced
1½ pounds watermelon, meat seeded and julienned
1 pound jicama, peeled and julienned (using a mandoline)
½ cup julienned red onion
2 tablespoons chopped cilantro
Kosher salt and freshly ground black pepper, to taste
1 teaspoon Tabasco red pepper sauce

1. Combine the radishes, watermelon, jicama, onion and cilantro in a mixing bowl.

2. Season with salt and pepper, to taste, and Tabasco sauce. Toss gently. Refrigerate for 30 minutes to allow the flavors to marry.

watermelon soup

2 poblano chilies
2 teaspoons coriander seeds
10 cups seeded and cubed watermelon meat (about 10 pounds whole melon)
½ cup mineral or filtered water (such as Panna)
¼ cup freshly squeezed orange juice
2 tablespoons fresh lime juice
2 tablespoons sugar
2½ teaspoons kosher salt
1 handful chopped cilantro
1 handful chopped mint

1. Preheat oven to 400 degrees.

2. Place the poblano chilies on a baking sheet and roast in the 400-degree oven until charred on all sides, checking often and turning halfway through cooking (about 15-18 minutes total). Place the hot peppers in a bowl and cover with plastic wrap. When cool enough to handle, peel away the skin. Halve and seed the poblanos, and cut into ½-inch cubes. Set aside.

3. Dry roast the coriander seeds by cooking them in a small skillet over low heat for about 4 minutes, shaking the pan.

4. In a food processor, puree the roasted coriander seeds, ½ of the watermelon, water, orange juice, 1 tablespoon of the lime juice, 1 tablespoon of the sugar and 1½ teaspoons of the salt. Transfer the mixture to a large bowl and add the rest of the watermelon cubes, roasted chilies, cilantro and mint. Adjust seasonings with the remaining 1 tablespoon lime juice, 1 tablespoon sugar and 1 teaspoon salt, or to taste. Mix well and refrigerate.

grilled chicken

Extra-virgin olive oil, as needed
4 6-ounce boneless, skinless chicken breasts, trimmed of any fat or sinew
Kosher salt and freshly ground black pepper, to taste

1. Preheat grill to high heat. Oil the grids so that the chicken will not stick.

2. Place the chicken breasts on a plate and lightly coat with oil; season with salt and pepper, to taste.

3. Place the breasts on the grill and cook about 3 minutes on each side; move the chicken from the hot spot on your grill to a lower temperature area and cook until the internal temperature registers 160 degrees. Remove and let rest until cool enough to handle. Slice each breast into 5 strips.

assembly

1. In each of 4 bowls, place the watermelon and jicama salad and top with the chicken strips. Surround with a ladleful of chilled watermelon soup.

Serves 4

Porcini-crusted New York strip steak with summer vegetables

This is a typical recipe here at R bistro. The center-of-the-plate item, a grilled steak, is simply cooked correctly and allowed to rest. To complete the dish, I like to toss potatoes and vegetables. This happens to include summer vegetables, but you can change the recipe seasonally to fit whatever is readily available at the time. A combination of fresh herbs such as thyme, Italian flat-leaf parsley and basil is always a delicious addition.

porcini-crusted strip steak

4 8-ounce New York strip steaks, trimmed
Kosher salt and freshly ground black pepper, to taste
**1-1½ ounces dried porcini mushrooms, ground to dust in a
  spice grinder**

1. Preheat grill to high heat.

2. Season the strip steaks with salt and pepper. Place the porcini dust on a plate and crust the steaks on both sides with the mushroom powder.

3. Grill the steaks to desired doneness (about 7 minutes per side for medium-rare, registering at about 130 degrees on an instant-read thermometer). (See Internal Temperatures for Cooking Meat on page 7.) Set aside.

summer vegetables

Kosher salt, to taste
1 pound wax beans, trimmed
½ pound fingerling potatoes
3 tablespoons vegetable oil
2 yellow squash, cut into ½-moon slices
2 zucchini, cut into ½-moon slices
1 red onion, julienned
1 pint cherry or grape tomatoes (both red and yellow)
Freshly ground black pepper, to taste
**Fresh chopped herbs, to taste (such as thyme, Italian
  flat-leaf parsley and basil)**
2 tablespoons unsalted butter

1. Bring a pot of salted water to a boil over high heat. Drop the trimmed beans into the boiling water to blanch (about 3-5 minutes). Drain and then plunge into an ice water bath to stop the cooking process; drain well and dry.

2. Place the potatoes in a 2-quart pot and cover with cold water; liberally salt the water. Bring to a boil and cook until just tender, and the edges are starting to soften. Drain well, allow to cool and then quarter.

3. To a large saute pan over medium-high heat, add the vegetable oil; once it is hot, saute the quartered fingerlings until golden (about 5 minutes), turning to cook evenly.

4. Add the squash, zucchini and red onion and cook until the vegetables are tender (about 8 minutes).

5. Gingerly fold in the beans and tomatoes and cook until everything is heated through (about 3 more minutes). Season with salt and pepper, to taste, and then add the fresh herbs and butter, which will give the vegetables a nice gloss.

assembly

1. To serve, place the vegetables in the center of each of 4 plates and angle a New York strip over the vegetables.

Serves 4

"Try this with vanilla ice crear

Blackberry pie with vanilla ice cream

This is a great pie recipe that holds its shape when sliced. I snagged the recipe from my friend Gail Smith who owns Almost Home restaurant in Greencastle, Indiana. Try this with vanilla ice cream, and you will be hooked!

pastry crust (yields 2 crusts)

8 ounces all-purpose flour, sifted
2 tablespoons confectioners' sugar, sifted
1 pinch salt
4 ounces unsalted butter, cut into cubes
1 egg, slightly beaten
1 tablespoon ice water

1. Keeping everything as cool as possible, sieve the flour, sugar and salt into a bowl; rub the butter cubes into the dry mixture with your fingertips. When the mixture looks like coarse bread crumbs, stop.

2. In a separate bowl, whisk together the egg and water. Using a pastry blender, add just enough of the liquid to the dry ingredients to bring the pastry together. Collect the pastry into a ball with your hands; this will help you judge more accurately if you need additional liquid. Gently pat the dough into 2 discs; wrap them separately in plastic and refrigerate for 1 hour.

3. Flour your work surface and gingerly roll out 1 of the pastry dough discs. Line a 9-inch pie pan with the dough (do not trim the edges). Place in freezer until ready to bake. (This will help prevent the crust from shrinking during baking.)

4. Roll out the other disc (large enough to cover the 9-inch pie) and place on a sheet pan; refrigerate.

filling

1¾ cups granulated sugar
1½ tablespoons granular tapioca
3½ tablespoons cornstarch
1 pinch salt
¼ teaspoon ground cinnamon
2 teaspoons fresh lemon juice
4 cups fresh or frozen blackberries, thawed
Unsalted butter, as needed

1. In a mixing bowl, combine the sugar, tapioca, cornstarch, salt and cinnamon.

2. Add in the lemon juice and blackberries and toss well.

3. Pour into the chilled pie shell. Dot the top with butter.

assembly

¼ cup heavy cream
Granulated sugar, to taste
Vanilla ice cream, to serve

1. Preheat oven to 425 degrees. Moisten the lip of the bottom crust with water.

2. Place the top crust over the filling. Trim the edges and seal the crusts well by fluting them. Brush the pastry top with cream and sprinkle with sugar, to taste. Cut 6 large vents in the top crust near the center.

3. Place the pie pan on a sheet pan. Bake in the 425-degree oven for 20 minutes.

4. Reduce oven temperature to 350 degrees and bake an additional 40 minutes or until golden brown. Remove and allow the pie to cool.

5. Slice the pie and serve in bowls with a scoop of vanilla ice cream.

Serves 8

Peach praline pie with vanilla ice cream

Here is a delicious summertime recipe for peach pie, perfect when the fruit is at its peak. Like the blackberry pie on page 57, my friend Gail Smith shared this recipe with me.

pastry crust (yields 2 crusts)

8 ounces all-purpose flour, sifted
2 tablespoons confectioners' sugar, sifted
1 pinch salt
4 ounces unsalted butter, cut into cubes
1 egg, slightly beaten
1 tablespoon ice water

1. Keeping everything as cool as possible, sieve the flour, sugar and salt into a bowl; rub the butter cubes into the dry mixture with your fingertips. When the mixture looks like coarse bread crumbs, stop.

2. In a separate bowl, whisk together the egg and water. Using a pastry blender, add just enough of the liquid to the dry ingredients to bring the pastry together. Collect the pastry into a ball with your hands; this will help you judge more accurately if you need additional liquid. Gently pat the dough into 2 discs; wrap them separately in plastic and refrigerate for 1 hour.

3. Flour your work surface and gingerly roll out 1 of the pastry dough discs.* Line a 9-inch tart pan and trim the edges. Place in freezer until ready to bake. (This will help prevent the crust from shrinking during baking.)

filling

6-8 peaches, pitted, peeled and sliced
½ cup granulated sugar
1 tablespoon granular tapioca
1 teaspoon lemon juice
½ teaspoon ground cinnamon

1. Toss together all of the filling ingredients. Set aside.

topping

½ cup all-purpose flour
½ cup chopped nuts (such as pecans or walnuts)
¼ cup unsalted butter
½ cup granulated sugar

1. In a food processor, process the topping ingredients until the mixture is crumbly.

assembly

Vanilla ice cream, to serve

1. Preheat oven to 350 degrees.

2. Sprinkle half of the topping mixture onto the bottom of the chilled pastry. Add the filling; top with the remaining topping.

3. Place the pie on a sheet pan and bake for 1¼-1½ hours or until juicy and bubbly. Remove and allow the pie to cool.

4. Cut the pie into 8 pieces and serve with a scoop of vanilla ice cream.

Serves 8

*Save the second pastry crust disc for another pie. Freeze, and then thaw and roll out to use.

autumn

With the first cool evening in September, I'm ready to pull on a sweater and welcome autumn. It's time to nest once again, enjoying warming soups and braises while the wind rustles the leaves outside.

This time of the year reminds me of apple cider reductions, pumpkins for roasting and winter squash to be used now and on into winter. Here is a colorful collection of some more unusual dishes.

Smoked salmon with avocado and apricot relish on potato pancake

This is a popular first course item at R bistro. I used this pancake recipe when I worked in North Yorkshire, England, back in the late 1990s. It's very consistent in texture. The relish is basic, and I made it up along the way. Crème fraîche is probably easier to make than it is to find in the grocery store, so it's just a matter of planning ahead. The salmon that I prefer to use in this dish is cold-smoked with a delicate texture.

apricot relish

1 pound dried apricots, chopped
2 small shallots, minced
1 cup black currants
1 star anise
2 tablespoons sherry vinegar
2 tablespoons sugar
1 pinch salt

1. Combine all of the apricot relish ingredients in a 2-quart saucepan and bring to a boil.

2. Cook until reduced to a slightly thicker consistency (about 10-15 minutes). Cool and refrigerate for up to 1 week.

potato pancake

Kosher salt, to taste
1 pound floury potatoes, such as Idaho bakers
3 eggs plus the whites of 2 more eggs
3 heaping tablespoons self-rising flour
5 ounces (just under ¾ cup) milk
5 ounces (just under ¾ cup) heavy cream
1 teaspoon freshly grated nutmeg
Freshly ground black pepper, to taste
About 4 tablespoons vegetable oil

1. On the day before you plan to serve, place a pan of salted water over high heat. Peel the potatoes and cut them up into large dice. Boil them until they are tender (8-15 minutes).

2. Drain the potatoes at once in a colander. Return them to the hot pan and mash them thoroughly or put them through a mouli or ricer. Do this dry (don't add any butter, cream or milk). Store the potatoes in a covered bowl in the refrigerator overnight (don't keep them for more than 24 hours, or they will blacken as they oxidize).

3. The next day, beat the 3 whole eggs and the flour into the mashed potatoes. Set aside.

4. In a small pan, combine the milk and cream over medium-high heat to scald, just shy of a boil.

5. Whisk the milk mixture into the potatoes until a thick batter is produced. Grate in the nutmeg and season with salt and pepper, to taste.

6. Whip the egg whites with a whisk or handheld mixer until they hold a stiff peak. With a rubber spatula, gingerly fold the whites into the batter. (Don't worry if the resulting batter is lightly striped with whites; they keep the pancakes light and airy.)

7. Heat a large skillet with 1 tablespoon of the oil over medium-low heat for 1-2 minutes. When the oil is hot, begin to spoon the batter into the hot skillet, making pancakes about 3 inches in diameter. After a couple of minutes, when the bottoms of the pancakes have browned, flip them and cook another 2 minutes on the other side. Add more oil as needed as you cook the rest of pancakes.

8. Transfer the pancakes to a wire rack to cool.

crème fraîche

1 cup whipping cream
1 tablespoon buttermilk

1. On the day before, make the crème fraîche by mixing together the cream and buttermilk in a glass bowl. Cover the bowl and allow the mixture to sit overnight on the counter.

assembly

1 avocado, quartered and then sliced
Red wine vinaigrette (see recipe on page 52)
6-8 slices smoked salmon (1½ slices per person)
1 bunch chives, chopped, to garnish

1. Warm the potato pancakes in the microwave for about 20 seconds. Set up 4 plates and place 2 overlapping pancakes in the center of each plate. Dip the avocado slices in a little of the vinaigrette and arrange on the pancakes. Top with about 1 tablespoon apricot relish. (An alternative presentation with the avocado on top of the relish appears in the photo on page 62.)

2. Attractively arrange the smoked salmon on top of the relish. Top with a dollop of crème fraîche and then sprinkle with chives.

Serves 4

Pâté of the South: pimento cheese and house-made flatbread

A recipe from Louis Osteen, a low-country chef in Charleston, South Carolina, inspired this pimento cheese recipe. Once you make this, you will never purchase it again at the grocery store. The flatbread pairs nicely with the cheese spread as well as the celery. This pimento cheese can be served as individual appetizers or in a large bowl for parties. Spread it on toast with tomato and lettuce to make a delicious sandwich.

pimento cheese

1½ pounds sharp cheddar cheese, grated
4 ounces cream cheese, room temperature
¾ cup mayonnaise (Hellman's preferred)
1 tablespoon grated yellow onion
⅛ teaspoon cayenne pepper, or to taste
**7 ounces whole peeled pimentos, drained and chopped
   (or roasted red peppers)**

1. Place the cheddar cheese, cream cheese, mayonnaise, onion and cayenne pepper in the bowl of an electric mixer and beat with the flat beater attachment 1-2 minutes on medium speed. You only want to mix the ingredients, not make them smooth.

2. Add the pimentos and continue mixing until they are mixed through, and the mixture is somewhat smooth. Be careful not to overmix.

3. Pack the cheese into small ramekins. Cover with plastic wrap and refrigerate overnight.

4. Remove from the refrigerator at least 45 minutes before serving. (Tightly covered, it will keep in the refrigerator 1 week.)

flatbread (makes 8 large pieces)

2 cups all-purpose flour, plus more as needed
2 tablespoons sesame seeds (1 tablespoon white and
**   1 tablespoon black seeds)**
1 tablespoon kosher salt
¼ teaspoon freshly ground black pepper
¾ cup warm water

1. Preheat oven to 400 degrees.

2. Combine the 2 cups flour, sesame seeds, salt and pepper in the bowl of an electric mixer. Using the flat beater attachment with the mixer on medium speed, slowly add the water and mix the dough for about 5 minutes or until it comes together and forms a ball.

3. Turn the dough out onto a floured surface and cut it into 8 equal pieces. Roll the pieces out in circles as thinly as possible; the shape isn't important, but the thinness is. Place the circles on ungreased baking sheets and prick them all over with the tines of a fork.

4. Bake the flatbread in the 400-degree oven 5-10 minutes. Turn the sheets over and continue to bake until the bread is golden brown, blistered and crispy (another 5-10 minutes). Cool and store in a covered container.

assembly

1 head celery, washed, strings removed and cut into
**   slender sticks**

1. Place a ramekin of pimento cheese in the center of a dinner plate or appetizer plate. Break the flatbread into usable pieces and arrange around the ramekin. Serve with celery sticks as well.

Yields about 4 cups pimento cheese

"This is a fu

Margarita scallops

This is a fun recipe, and it presents well in salt-rimmed cocktail glasses. A great starter for a Tex-Mex meal, I adapted the recipe from a cookbook I picked up in Arizona.

¼ cup tequila
1 cup freshly squeezed lime juice
½ cup freshly squeezed lemon juice
½ cup sugar
1-2 jalapeños, stemmed, seeded and coarsely chopped, plus more to taste
1 green onion, cut into ½- to ¾-inch pieces
1 cup chopped cilantro leaves plus 3 teaspoons minced cilantro, to garnish
1 teaspoon chopped garlic
½ teaspoon salt, plus more as needed
1 tablespoon vegetable oil
¾ pound sea scallops (3 per person, 10-20 count)
1 lime, quartered

1. Place the first 9 ingredients (tequila, lime juice, lemon juice, sugar, jalapeños, green onion, 1 cup chopped cilantro, garlic and salt) in a food processor and puree. Taste the mixture and add more jalapeños, to taste. Transfer to a mixing bowl and set aside.

2. Wet the rims of 4 cocktail glasses and then dip in salt. Set them aside.

3. Per serving, drizzle a little oil into a saute pan over high heat. When it is just smoking, add 3 scallops and sear well (only about 1 minute). Before turning, deglaze the pan with ¼ cup margarita liquid. Turn the scallops and continue to cook until done (about 1 more minute).

4. Leaving the liquid in the pan to reduce, place 3 scallops in a glass. Once the liquid has reduced and thickened sufficiently, pour it over the scallops. Garnish with a lime wedge and minced cilantro. (An alternative presentation appears in the photo on page 66.)

Serves 4

Warm lump crabmeat on pickled red onions and roasted beets

I was in Louisville, Kentucky, for a Women's Chef & Restaurateurs annual meeting back in 2004 with my sous chef. We enjoyed a dish similar to this combination, and were inspired to create one of our own. I found a recipe for pickled red onions, and the crab combination is normally what I serve as a warm crab dip at parties. I've been using the dip since the early '90s and now call it my own.

beets

1 pound beets
Vegetable oil, as needed
Kosher salt and freshly ground black pepper, to taste

1. Preheat oven to 400 degrees.
2. Scrub the beets clean, rub them with a little oil and then sprinkle with salt and pepper, to taste. Place them in a deep roasting pan with a little water to cover the bottom and then seal with foil.
3. Place in the 400-degree oven and roast until tender or until a paring knife inserted comes out easily (about 1 hour). Allow them to cool and then peel them. Cut into ¼-inch-thick slices.

pickled red onions (yields about 2 cups)

½ cup red wine vinegar
½ cup dry red wine
½ cup sugar
1 tablespoon mustard seeds
2 tablespoons black peppercorns
1 pinch crushed red pepper flakes
2 tablespoons kosher salt
3 medium-size red onions, peeled and sliced into
¼-inch-thick rings (using a mandoline)

1. In a medium-size saucepan, combine all of the ingredients except the onions. Stir over low heat until the sugar has dissolved. Add the onions and bring the liquid to a boil, raising the heat as needed. Simmer for 5 minutes and then remove the pan from the heat and let cool completely.
2. Transfer the cooled onions (with liquid) to a sterilized glass jar or clean container. Cover tightly and store in the refrigerator for up to 2 weeks.

seasoned crabmeat

1 1-pound can lump crabmeat
8 ounces cream cheese
1 clove garlic, crushed
¼ cup mayonnaise (Hellman's preferred)
1 tablespoon whole-grain mustard
1 teaspoon grated onion
2 tablespoons dry vermouth
Lawry's Seasoned Salt, to taste
A few dashes Tabasco red pepper sauce
1 tablespoon chopped fresh chives
Juice of 1 lemon
A few dashes Worcestershire sauce

1. Heat all of the seasoned crabmeat ingredients in the top of a double boiler until well blended, and the cheese is melted. Adjust seasonings, to taste, and allow it to cool. (If needed, you may rewarm it a microwave to serve.)

assembly

Fresh dill, to garnish

1. Place 3 overlapping slices of beet in the center of each plate. Top with a few drained pickled onions.
2. Crown with about 2 ounces warm crabmeat. Garnish with fresh dill on top.

Serves 6

Chili-honey glazed shrimp over brown rice with black beans

This is a hearty dish of shrimp, beans and rice. The beans-and-rice combination came from my sister-in-law, but I decided to top it with the grilled shrimp. The glaze was inspired from a cookbook I picked up at the Phoenix Airport when I traveled through there a few years ago. The pairing is great!

chili-honey glaze (makes about 2¼ cups)

1 cup freshly squeezed orange juice
¾ cup honey
⅓ cup freshly squeezed lime juice
⅓ cup Dijon mustard
2 tablespoons paprika
1 tablespoon chopped garlic
2 tablespoons chili powder
2 teaspoons dried oregano
2 teaspoons salt
1 teaspoon black pepper
1 teaspoon white pepper

1. Combine all of the chili-honey glaze ingredients in a saucepan and simmer over medium heat until thick and reduced by half (10-12 minutes). Set aside.

black beans

1 cup dried black beans
1 tablespoon cumin
1 tablespoon dried oregano
2 celery ribs
½ onion
1 teaspoon salt

1. Soak the beans in water overnight.

2. Drain the beans. Cook them in fresh water with the cumin, oregano, celery and onion (according to package directions).

3. Five minutes before they are done, add the salt. Drain and allow to cool; discard the celery and onion.

brown rice

1 cup brown rice
2 cups water
Kosher salt, to taste
1 tablespoon unsalted butter

1. Rinse the rice in cold water.

2. Put all of the brown rice ingredients in a pot with a tight-fitting lid. Over high heat, bring to a boil. Stir once and then reduce heat to low; cover and simmer for about 40-45 minutes.

3. Check for doneness and stir. When the water is totally absorbed, and the rice is cooked through, drain it. Pour the rice out onto a baking sheet and let it cool.

sauce

2 tablespoons extra-virgin olive oil
1 onion, chopped
2 cloves garlic, minced
1 teaspoon cumin, plus more to taste
1 28-ounce can chopped tomatoes, with juice
Kosher salt and freshly ground black pepper, to taste
Fresh chopped oregano, to taste

1. In a Dutch oven over medium heat, add the oil and saute the onion until translucent. Add the garlic and cook through (about 3 minutes).

2. Dust the onion with 1 teaspoon cumin. Add the tomatoes and simmer for 10 minutes.

3. Add the black beans and continue to simmer an additional 10 minutes. Adjust the seasoning with cumin, salt and pepper, to taste. Add fresh oregano, to taste.

grilled shrimp

1 pound large shrimp (about 5-6 per person), thawed, peeled and deveined (tail on)
Vegetable oil, as needed
Bamboo skewers, soaked in water for 10 minutes

1. Slide the shrimp onto the skewers about 5-6 each, depending on size. (You may also put 3 shrimp on each skewer and serve 2 skewers per person.)

2. Preheat a grill to medium-high heat and oil your grates.

3. Working quickly, brush the shrimp with the chili-honey glaze and place on the grill (less than 1 minute per side) to sear. Turn and brush again so the shrimp are nicely glazed. (You can also broil the shrimp, glazing and turning as you cook them.)

assembly

Chopped green onions, to garnish (optional)

1. Reheat the brown rice in the microwave and divide among 4 serving bowls. Top with the black beans and sauce.

2. Angle the skewers of grilled shrimp on top of the beans. Garnish with chopped green onions, if desired.

Serves 4

Ruby red trout with wild rice succotash and Pernod sauce

I found this recipe for succotash in a cookbook featuring edamame. I added a few ingredients to round it out for color. The butter sauce is a classic preparation, finished with Pernod to give it a licorice flavor. I think the combination of the succotash, trout and sauce is a perfect pairing. Great when you are hosting a party, most everything could be made ahead, except the fish, which only takes a few minutes at the end.

wild rice succotash

2 ounces wild rice
1 tablespoon extra-virgin olive oil
½ pound mushrooms, sliced
½ tablespoon chopped garlic
2 tablespoons white wine
½ pound fresh sweet corn kernels (or frozen, thawed)
½ pound edamame
1 large tomato, peeled, seeded and diced
1 tablespoon fresh chopped tarragon
4 green onions, chopped
Kosher salt and freshly ground black pepper, to taste

1. Cook the wild rice according to package directions. Set aside.

2. To a large skillet over medium-high heat, add the oil. When it's hot, add the mushrooms and saute until just tender. Add the garlic and cook until the aroma develops, being careful not to burn it.

3. Deglaze the pan with the white wine and continue to cook until all of the liquid has evaporated. Remove from heat.

4. In a large bowl, combine the corn, edamame, tomato, cooked wild rice and mushrooms. Toss well and add the tarragon and green onions. Season with salt and pepper, to taste.

pernod butter sauce

2 tablespoons minced shallots
1 cup dry white wine
½ cup heavy cream
¾ cup unsalted butter, cut into ½-inch cubes
Kosher salt, to taste
1 tablespoon Pernod, or to taste

1. In a medium-size saucepan, combine the shallots and white wine over medium-high heat. Reduce to only a few tablespoons of liquid.

2. Add the cream and then reduce by half.

3. At very low heat with whisk in hand, start adding the butter a few pieces at a time, being sure that the mixture has emulsified after each addition of butter. Do not let the sauce boil. (I go back and forth between having the pan on and off the burner; this is a tricky part of making the sauce.) Remove from heat.

4. Add salt, to taste, and then add the Pernod, to taste. Be sure to keep it warm until ready to use.

ruby red trout

3 tablespoons vegetable oil
6-8 5-ounce trout filets, skin on
Kosher salt and freshly ground black pepper, to taste

1. To a large skillet over high heat, add the oil. Season the trout on both sides with salt and pepper, to taste.

2. When the oil is smoking, carefully place the trout, skin side down, into the skillet. You will immediately hear the saute sound. Do not move the trout around in the pan; let the skin get crispy, though you may lower the temperature to medium-high. Shake the skillet gently, and the trout will begin to come away from the pan. When this occurs, turn the fish and finish the cooking process. (The total cooking time should be about 6 minutes.) Touch the fish; if there is a gentle give, the fish is done.

assembly

1. Place a spoonful of wild rice succotash in the center of each serving plate. Top with the ruby red trout, skin side up. Drizzle with the Pernod butter sauce, a little on the fish and on the plate.

Serves 6-8

"With mushroom

Quesadilla of turkey and jack cheese with tomato salsa and avocado

Combined with mushrooms and sage, ground turkey works very well as a quesadilla filling. The salsa usually has a few basic components including lime juice, peppers, cilantro, onion and tomatoes, well seasoned with salt, pepper and a touch of sugar, adjusted to what you prefer. These quesadillas are an easy supper that can be prepared in advance.

tomato salsa

1 pound tomatoes, peeled and chopped
½ bunch cilantro, chopped
1 bunch green onions, chopped
1 yellow pepper, chopped
1 jalapeño, seeded and chopped
Juice of 2 limes
Sugar, to taste
Kosher salt and freshly ground black pepper, to taste

1. Combine all of the tomato salsa ingredients. Taste and adjust seasoning with more jalapeño, lime juice, sugar, salt or pepper, to taste.

turkey filling

1 Spanish onion, chopped
2 tablespoons vegetable oil
1 pound ground turkey
½ pound sliced white mushrooms
1 yellow pepper, diced
Fresh thyme, chopped, to taste
Fresh sage, chopped, to taste
Kosher salt and freshly ground black pepper, to taste

1. In a pan over medium heat, saute the onion in the oil until translucent.

2. Add the ground turkey and saute until cooked through (3-5 minutes).

3. Add the mushrooms and pepper, cooking until the vegetables are tender.

4. Toss in the herbs and season with salt and pepper, to taste. Cover and set aside, keeping warm. (You may also cook this a day ahead and reheat to serve.)

assembly

1 package 6-inch flour tortillas (about 10-12 per package)
8 ounces Monterey Jack cheese, grated
½ cup vegetable oil
½-1 cup sour cream
2 avocados, peeled and sliced (about ¼ avocado per person)

1. Preheat oven to 400 degrees.

2. Prepare the quesadillas by laying the tortillas out flat. Place the turkey filling on 1 half of each tortilla and then top with the cheese. Fold over and cover the filling. *

3. In a 10-inch skillet over medium-high heat, add about 1 tablespoon of the vegetable oil and swirl the pan. Cooking one at a time, carefully place the quesadillas in the oil and brown on each side. Once a quesadilla is browned, place it in the 400-degree oven to warm through (about 2 minutes); remove from oven. Add more oil to the pan as needed to cook all of the quesadillas.

4. Cut each quesadilla into 3 pieces. (One quesadilla would be a perfect snack or enough for an appetizer.)

5. To serve, place a spoonful of the tomato salsa, a dollop of sour cream and a quarter of an avocado (sliced) on a plate with 3 wedges of quesadilla.

Serves about 6

* If you're doing this in advance, individually wrap the assembled quesadillas in plastic wrap; refrigerate and then pull out from the refrigerator, cooking 1 at a time.

Chicken breast topped with warm mushrooms, leeks and goat cheese over dressed mixed greens

This is a lunch salad that I've been serving during the cooler months over the last several years. I change my lunch menu seasonally, and this is a perfect autumn salad. You have the freshly cooked chicken for protein over leaves tossed in red wine vinaigrette. Then in a skillet, you saute the mushrooms and leeks until tender and add some goat cheese to soften. Once it's creamy, you spoon it over the chicken and leaves for a combination of hot and cold — a warming salad experience.

chicken

**4 6-ounce boneless, skinless chicken breasts, trimmed of
    fat and sinew**
Vegetable oil, as needed
Kosher salt and freshly ground black pepper, to taste

1. Place the chicken breasts on a plate and drizzle with oil; rub to coat on both sides. Season with salt and pepper, to taste.

2. Heat a saute pan over medium-high heat and add additional oil (enough to coat the bottom of the pan). When the pan is hot, carefully place the chicken breasts in it and saute until browned on one side; turn over and finish cooking until the juices run clear when a small knife is inserted (about 6-8 minutes). Remove from the saute pan to a cutting board and let rest for a few minutes until the dish is completed. Slice the breast into 5 pieces.

red wine vinaigrette

⅓ cup red wine vinegar
1 teaspoon sugar, or to taste
Kosher salt and freshly ground black pepper, to taste
1 tablespoon Dijon mustard
⅔ cup oil (half extra-virgin olive and half vegetable oil)

1. Whisk together all of the ingredients except oils.

2. Slowly drizzle in the oils, whisking constantly to emulsify. Set aside.

salad

4 handfuls mixed lettuce leaves (your choice)

1. Lightly dress the mixed greens with the red wine vinaigrette, toss and set aside.

mushroom and leek saute

¼ cup shelled hazelnuts
4 tablespoons extra-virgin olive oil
½ pound white mushrooms, sliced
**½ pound assorted mushrooms, torn into pieces (such as
    oyster, shiitake and crimini)**
1 leek, trimmed, rinsed of sand and cut into ½-inch moons
A few tablespoons white wine, or as needed
Kosher salt and freshly ground black pepper, to taste
4 ounces goat cheese, portioned into 1-ounce pieces

1. Preheat oven to 400 degrees. Place the hazelnuts on a sheet pan. Toast the nuts in the 400-degree oven until they are lightly colored, and the skins have loosened. Remove the nuts from the oven and wrap them in a kitchen towel for 1 minute. Rub them in the towel to remove the loose skins. Allow them to cool and then roughly chop.

2. In a saute pan over medium-high heat, add the olive oil and swirl the pan. Saute the mushrooms and leek until softened (about 5-8 minutes).

3. Add the hazelnuts and deglaze the pan with white wine, scraping up any bits stuck to the bottom of the pan; toss to incorporate. Season with salt and pepper, to taste. Place 4 pieces of goat cheese on top of the mushroom mixture and let them melt slightly.

assembly

1. Divide the dressed greens among 4 cold plates. Top with the sliced chicken and then carefully spoon the mushroom and leek saute on top of the chicken along with the warmed goat cheese.

Serves 4

Quail and sausage braised with grapes, with blue cheese and walnut polenta

This quail dish was inspired by a recipe from Judy Rodgers of The Zuni Café in San Francisco. I have gotten a lot of ideas from her cookbook, and the grapes in this dish are beautiful. I've been doing the polenta combination for years, even as a passed hors d'oeuvre.

polenta with blue cheese and walnuts

½ cup walnut halves
4 cups water
1 teaspoon salt
1 cup cornmeal
½ cup freshly grated Parmesan
3 tablespoons unsalted butter
3 tablespoons chopped parsley
Kosher salt and freshly ground black pepper, to taste
½ cup Danish blue cheese crumbles

1. Preheat oven to 400 degrees. Place the walnuts on a small sheet tray and toast them in the 400-degree oven until golden (check in after about 3 minutes and shake the pan for even toasting). Remove them from the oven, allow to cool and then chop.

2. In a medium-size pot over high heat, bring the water and salt to a boil. While whisking constantly, add the cornmeal in a steady stream.

3. Lower the heat and add the Parmesan, butter, parsley and salt and pepper, to taste. Switch to a rubber scraper to stir; continue to cook at a gentle simmer until the cornmeal is creamy and pulls away from the sides of the pot. If the polenta gets too thick, add additional water and mix well.

4. Prepare a sheet pan with cooking spray. Pour the polenta onto the sheet pan and smooth out with the rubber scraper to make even. Sprinkle the polenta with the blue cheese and walnuts and then lightly pat to ensure the ingredients are in the polenta firmly. Cool and refrigerate.

5. Cut the polenta into 3" x 3" squares and remove from the pan. Place 4 on a plate and warm in the microwave. (Refrigerate the remaining polenta and use for a midnight snack.)

quail and sausage with grapes

¼ cup plus 2 tablespoons extra-virgin olive oil
A few pinches fennel seeds, barely crushed
2 pounds small red or black seedless grapes
Kosher salt, to taste
Balsamic or red wine vinegar, as needed
4 whole quail, partially boned
4 3-ounce fresh sausages (fennel sausage preferred)*
Freshly ground black pepper, to taste

1. Warm about ¼ cup olive oil with the fennel seeds in a 3-quart saute pan over medium heat.

2. Add the grapes. Stir regularly until the skins begin to split, and the grapes yield their juice. Cook, stirring occasionally, until the sauce has a little body (20-30 minutes). You should have about 2 cups. If the grapes are quite sweet, add a small pinch salt and/or dribble of vinegar. Set aside.

3. Into a 12-inch skillet over medium heat, drizzle about 2 tablespoons olive oil.

4. Season the quail and sausages with salt and pepper, to taste, and then place them in the pan. Brown them evenly (3-4 minutes on each side). Reduce the heat and tilt the pan, trapping the quail and sausages behind tongs or a strainer; pour off the excess fat.

5. Add the grapes to the dish. Cover and cook over medium-low heat until the quail is firm, like a ripe peach (an additional 10-12 minutes or so), turning the quail and sausages a few times to ensure even cooking. Uncover and simmer to reduce the sauce to a rich, jammy consistency. Taste and correct with salt and vinegar.

assembly

Fennel fronds, to garnish

1. For each of 4 servings, place a piece of polenta at the top of each plate and top with the quail, a sausage and then cascade the grape sauce onto the quail. Garnish with a fennel frond.

Serves 4

*I prefer to use loose sausage and then season it with fennel seed and shape it into 2-ounce patties. Sausage links, as shown in the photo on page 78, make quick work of the recipe.

Sumac-rubbed loin of lamb with flageolet beans

My friend Jana brought me a gift of sumac, so I had to come up with a way to use this tangy spice. We combined it with a few other spices and made a rub for lamb loin, served over a colorful toss of beans, tomatoes, onions and walnuts — as the starch — with some Swiss chard to finish.

spice rub

1 large pinch sumac
¼ teaspoon ground cinnamon
1 large pinch cayenne pepper or chili pepper

1. Combine all of the spice rub ingredients. Taste and adjust seasonings as needed.

loin of lamb

4 5-ounce lamb loins, trimmed of excess fat and sinew
Kosher salt, to taste

1. Preheat grill to medium-high heat.

2. Sprinkle the lamb loins with the spice rub and salt and then grill them to medium-rare (about 3 minutes per side). (See Internal Temperatures for Cooking Meat on page 7.) Allow them to rest for a few minutes and then slice into 5 pieces. Set aside.

green flageolet bean toss

1 cup shelled walnuts, to garnish
2 tablespoons extra-virgin olive oil
½ onion, diced
2-3 cloves garlic, minced
1 pound dried flageolet beans, cooked according to package directions*
½ pound Roma tomatoes, peeled, seeded and chopped
Kosher salt and freshly ground black pepper, to taste
½ bunch cilantro, leaves finely chopped

1. Preheat oven to 400 degrees. Place the walnuts on a small sheet tray and toast them in the 400-degree oven until golden (check i after about 3 minutes and shake the pan for even toasting). Remove from the oven, allow to cool and then coarsely chop.

2. Pour the olive oil into a large saute pan over medium-low heat and cook the onion very gently until translucent (about 8 minutes).

3. Add the garlic, beans and tomatoes to the pan and mix well to warm through. Season with salt and pepper, to taste.

4. Stir in the cilantro. Garnish with the walnuts to serve. (This may be reheated with a little chicken stock, if needed.)

Swiss chard

1½ pounds Swiss chard, washed well and drained
1 tablespoon vegetable oil
1 tablespoon unsalted butter
Kosher salt and freshly ground black pepper, to taste
2 tablespoons sherry vinegar

1. Cut the stems and thick center ribs from the Swiss chard leaves. Discard the center ribs; coarsely chop the stems and cut the leaves into chiffonade (ribbon-like strips).

2. In a large saute pan over medium-high heat, add the oil and butter and then the stems; saute a few minutes.

3. Add the leaves and saute until wilted; season with salt and pepper, to taste.

4. Add the vinegar and toss. Remove from heat.

assembly

1. Place the green flageolet bean toss in the center of each plate with the Swiss chard.

2. Top with fanned lamb loin slices. (An alternative presentation appears in the photo on page 80.)

Serves 4

*If flageolet beans are unavailable, choose very small dried white beans.

Grilled veal chops with vegetable hash and horseradish

This recipe is a combination of ideas. For the marinade, it's best to use fresh herbs. White wine and a little honey help to balance the flavors. Be sure to taste this before you put in the chops to marinate. The vegetable hash is a last-minute saute made as the chops are grilling. I prepare this dish in autumn and winter, when these vegetables are readily available. I think I found the horseradish sauce recipe on the Food Network Web site and knew that it would complete the dish.

horseradish sauce

3 tablespoons prepared horseradish
¼ cup sour cream
1 teaspoon Dijon mustard
1 tablespoon mayonnaise
1 tablespoon chopped chives

1. Mix together all of the horseradish sauce ingredients. Refrigerate until service.

marinated, grilled veal chops

½ cup extra-virgin olive oil
1 cup white wine
1 tablespoon finely chopped sage
1 tablespoon chopped fresh thyme
1 tablespoon finely chopped Italian flat-leaf parsley
1 tablespoon freshly ground black pepper
1 tablespoon honey
4 8- to 12-ounce veal chops
Vegetable oil, as needed
Kosher salt, to taste

1. Combine all of the marinade ingredients (first 7 ingredients). Place the veal chops in a flat container and pour the marinade over them. Allow the veal to marinate in the refrigerator 3-6 hours.

2. Preheat grill to high heat. Oil the racks to prevent the veal from sticking.

3. Remove the chops from the marinade, season with salt and place on the grill. Cook the chops 7-9 minutes on each side, until internal temperature is 135 degrees on an instant-read thermometer for medium-rare doneness. (See Internal Temperatures for Cooking Meat on page 7.) Remove from heat and allow the veal to rest for at least 5 minutes.

vegetable hash

2 medium-size beets (with their greens)
Kosher salt, to taste
1 pound fingerling potatoes
3 cloves garlic, peeled

Vegetable oil, as needed
1 onion, small dice
1 carrot, grated
About 4 tablespoons unsalted butter, diced
¼ cup fresh chopped herbs (such as parsley and chives)
Freshly ground black pepper, to taste
About 6 ounces cheddar cheese, grated

1. Roast the beets. To do so, preheat oven to 400 degrees. Trim the greens and most of the stems from the beets. Wrap each in foil and roast directly on the oven rack until fork tender (about 1 hour, depending on the size of the beets). Allow them to cool, peel them and then dice.

2. Bring a pot of salted water to a boil over high heat. Drop the fingerlings into the boiling water to blanch (about 5 minutes). Drain and then plunge into an ice water bath to stop the cooking process; drain well. When they are cool enough to handle, dice them.

3. Bring a small saucepan of water to a boil over high heat. Drop the peeled garlic cloves into the boiling water to blanch (about 3 minutes). Drain and then refresh under cold running water; drain well. When they are cool enough to handle, thinly slice.

4. In a small saute pan over medium-high heat, begin with a little vegetable oil and saute the onion and fingerlings just until the onion is fragrant; add the carrot and beets, sauteing for another minute. Add the garlic. Cook until the fingerlings are cooked through and then add a little butter and the fresh herbs; season with salt and pepper, to taste. Finish with a little cheddar cheese to help bind and toss.

assembly

1. Place the vegetable hash in the center of each plate and top with a grilled veal chop. Place a dollop of the sauce alongside the hash.

Serves 4

Meatballs with ricotta in broth with green sauce

This is a delightful soup, probably one of the few that I have written down. The meatballs are a combination of pork and turkey, but you could also use lamb or beef. The pistachios and cornichons give them a little crunch. This idea is a combination of several recipes for the meatballs; try using ricotta in your regular meatballs to make them more tender and lighter. The green sauce is fairly simple. Use any variety of fresh/cooked vegetables; this is a tasty soup that could be a meal.

meatballs

½ pound ground pork
½ pound ground turkey
½ pound ricotta cheese
2 large eggs, beaten
¼ cup freshly grated Parmesan cheese
¼ cup fresh bread crumbs
6 cornichons, chopped
3 ounces shelled pistachio nuts, chopped
3 tablespoons unsalted butter
2 cups chicken stock, or as needed
Kosher salt and freshly ground black pepper, to taste

1. In a large bowl, combine the ground meats, ricotta, eggs, Parmesan, bread crumbs, cornichons and pistachios and mix well with your hands just until blended. Form into balls 1 inch in diameter. (Cook off a small meatball to be sure the meat is well seasoned.)

2. In a large heavy-bottomed pot, heat the butter over medium heat until it foams and then subsides. Place the meatballs in the pan and brown on all sides. Add the stock; the liquid should come halfway up the sides of the pot, being sure to cover the meatballs. Bring to a boil, and then reduce to a simmer and cook until the meatballs are cooked through (about 15 minutes). Season the broth with salt and pepper, to taste. Remove the meatballs and cool separately. Reserve the broth.

salsa verde

1 bunch Italian flat-leaf parsley, leaves only
4 salt-packed anchovies, filleted and rinsed
1 bunch mint, leaves only
Fronds from 1 fennel bulb
2 tablespoons capers
1 hard-boiled egg, roughly chopped

4 cornichons
2 tablespoons white wine vinegar
1 cup extra-virgin olive oil
Freshly ground black pepper, to taste

1. Combine all of the ingredients in a food processor and blend until smooth. Adjust seasonings, to taste.

vegetables

Any vegetables of your choice would work for the soup. Here are a few examples that taste great, or use a variety of the three different choices. Just have them ready to go and add to the soup in the final stages.

2 cups green beans, diced and blanched
1 large onion, chopped and sauteed in butter
2 cups diced carrots, blanched
(Other options include zucchini, fava beans, edamame, corn and diced tomatoes)

assembly

2 hard-boiled eggs, chopped (½ egg per person)
Asiago bread, sliced, brushed with extra-virgin olive oil and grilled in a grill pan (2 slices per person)

1. Ladle the reserved broth (from meatballs recipe at left) into a 3-quart pot and add about 20 meatballs and enough vegetables for 4 portions. Bring the mixture to a boil and then ladle the soup into 4 bowls (with 5 meatballs per person).

2. Garnish with the chopped egg and drizzle generously with the salsa verde. Serve with grilled Asiago bread.

Serves 4

Toffeed apple and pecan tart

This recipe is from a seasonal dessert cookbook I purchased while living in England. If you don't have one, a scale with both ounces and grams is a great tool to own. That way you'll have the ability to make any recipe from around the world. This is a good recipe in autumn. The tart tastes best if made on the day of serving but at least 3 hours in advance, giving you time to chill it in the refrigerator. This firms up the filling, giving it a toffee-like quality.

pastry crust (yields 2 crusts)

8 ounces all-purpose flour, sifted, plus more as needed
2 tablespoons confectioners' sugar, sifted
1 pinch salt
4 ounces unsalted butter, cubed
1 egg, slightly beaten
1 tablespoon ice water

1. Keeping everything as cool as possible, sieve the flour, sugar and salt into a bowl; rub the butter cubes into the dry mixture with your fingertips. When the mixture looks like coarse bread crumbs, stop.

2. In a separate bowl, whisk together the egg and water. Using a pastry blender, add just enough of the liquid to the dry ingredients to bring the pastry together. Collect the pastry into a ball with your hands; this will help you judge more accurately if you need additional liquid. Gently pat the dough into 2 discs; wrap them separately in plastic and refrigerate for 1 hour.

3. Flour your work surface and gingerly roll out 1 of the pastry dough discs.* Line a 9-inch tart pan and trim the edges. Place in a freezer until ready to bake. (This will help prevent the crust from shrinking during baking.)

4. Preheat oven to 400 degrees.

5. Blind bake the pastry crust by lining the chilled tart pan with aluminum foil and then placing pie weights or dried beans in the tart, being sure to arrange them to all ends of the tart. Bake in the 400-degree oven for 15 minutes and check for doneness. Remove the foil and weights and check for transparency. Bake for another minute or 2, and then remove when just golden and dry looking. Allow to cool.

filling

5 ounces (1 stick plus 2 tablespoons) unsalted butter
5 ounces light brown sugar
3 ounces heavy cream
5 ounces pecan halves
2 small Granny Smith apples
2 eggs, beaten
Whipped cream, to garnish

1. Preheat oven to 350 degrees.

2. Place the butter, sugar and cream in a saucepan large enough to hold all of the filling ingredients. Cook slowly to dissolve the sugar; bring to a boil and cook, stirring, for 1 minute. Remove from the heat and stir in the pecans. Allow to cool slightly.

3. Peel and core the apples and cut into ½-inch dice. Stir into the toffee mixture along with the beaten eggs.

4. Spoon into the pastry crust and bake in the 350-degree oven 20-25 minutes. Remove from the oven and allow to cool before serving. Serve with a dollop of whipped cream.

Serves 8

*Save the second pastry crust disc for another pie. Freeze, and then thaw and roll out to use.

My mother's cheesecake

This is my mother's cheesecake recipe that is very rich and creamy. I love it! The sour cream topping creates a tangy, sweet layer that presents beautifully.

crust

14 graham crackers
2 tablespoons sugar
⅓ cup melted unsalted butter

1. In a food processor, blend together all of the crust ingredients and spread evenly on the bottom of a 13" x 9" x 2" cake or lasagna pan.

cheesecake

24 ounces cream cheese, room temperature
1 cup sugar
5 eggs
1½ teaspoons pure vanilla extract

1. Preheat oven to 325 degrees.
2. In the bowl of an electric mixer, add the cheese and sugar and beat until smooth.
3. With the mixer running, add the eggs 1 at a time and then the vanilla, being sure it is all well-blended with no lumps. Pour over the crust.
4. Bake in the 325-degree oven for 45-60 minutes.

sour cream topping

1 pint sour cream
2 tablespoons sugar
3 teaspoons vanilla

1. Combine all of the topping ingredients until smooth.
2. When the cake has cooked 1 hour, remove it from the oven and reduce oven temperature to 300 degrees. Spread the sour cream topping evenly over the top of the cake. Return it to the oven and bake 5-8 minutes (do not let it brown). Remove, allow it to cool and then refrigerate to chill.
3. Slice into small squares and serve.

Serves 12

winter

Warm up your kitchen and cater to cold weather's heartier appetites by slow cooking and roasting meats.

Savor robust flavors of beef tenderloin and tender veal, a celery root puree with earthy French lentils, and don't forget the red velvet cake for dessert. With winter's packed schedule of holidays, there are plenty of opportunities to put your best dishes forward.

Lamb and feta quesadilla with lingonberry and toasted hazelnut salsa

This lingonberry salsa presents with great color. I originally saw the recipe utilizing duck, but I wanted to use lamb and French feta, so this is my version of the quesadilla.

lingonberry hazelnut salsa

½ **cup hazelnuts**
2 cups prepared lingonberry sauce
2 tablespoons seeded and finely diced jalapeño peppers,
   or to taste
½ **cup small-dice red onion**
3 tablespoons finely chopped cilantro
Kosher salt and freshly ground black pepper, to taste

1. Preheat oven to 400 degrees. Place the hazelnuts on a small sheet tray. Toast the nuts in the 400-degree oven until golden. Check after 3 minutes and watch carefully until lightly toasted. Remove from the oven, allow to cool and roughly chop.

2. Combine all of the lingonberry hazelnut salsa ingredients. Cover and refrigerate until needed.

caramelized onions

2 tablespoons vegetable oil
3 large onions, thinly sliced

1. In a large saute pan, heat the oil over medium-high heat. Add the onions and slowly caramelize until they are brown and creamy (about 20 minutes). These need to be watched carefully so that they do not burn; turn down the heat if needed and stir occasionally. If the onions are sticking to the pan, add a little water to loosen them and continue to brown.

2. Remove from heat and place in a bowl; set aside.

lamb loins

1 pound lamb loin, trimmed of fat and silver skin
Kosher salt and freshly ground black pepper, to taste
1 tablespoon vegetable oil

1. Cut the lamb into 6 pieces all about the same weight; season with salt and pepper, to taste.

2. Heat a skillet with the vegetable oil and swirl. Add the lamb pieces and sear on all sides until nicely browned.

3. Remove the lamb from the pan and let rest. Slice each piece into 6 thin slices; set aside.

assembly

12 6-inch flour tortillas
12 ounces French (or Greek) feta cheese, crumbled
Vegetable oil, as needed
1 package mesclun leaves, to garnish
Extra-virgin olive oil, as needed

1. Preheat oven to 400 degrees.

2. On each tortilla, sprinkle crumbled feta on the bottom half and then top with 1 tablespoon onions and 3 slices lamb; fold over. Place on a parchment-lined sheet pan. Continue this process with each of the 12 tortillas. (Wrap 6 in plastic wrap and refrigerate for a midnight snack.)

3. In a 10-inch skillet over medium-high heat, add about 1 tablespoon vegetable oil and swirl the pan. One at a time, carefully place the quesadillas in the oil and brown on each side. Once a quesadilla is browned, return it to the sheet pan and the 400-degree oven to warm through (about 2 minutes). Remove from oven. Cut each quesadilla into 4 wedges.

4. On each plate, place a dollop of the lingonberry hazelnut salsa, a few mesclun leaves tossed in olive oil for shine and the wedges of quesadilla.

Serves 6 or 12

Seared beef tenderloin bruschetta with roasted peppers and red onions on Asiago bread and arugula salad

This colorful dish is very simple to make. You can prepare it in advance and then compose it right before serving. Bruschetta were very popular in the mid-'90s, so I was always thinking of what to use as components. We may have used this combination or a similar idea while I was working at the Yorke Arms in North Yorkshire.

beef tenderloin

1 pound beef tenderloin, trimmed of fat and silver skin, kept in 1 piece
Extra-virgin olive oil, as needed
Kosher salt and freshly ground black pepper, to taste
Vegetable oil, as needed

1. Preheat oven to 400 degrees.
2. Rub the beef with olive oil all over and then season liberally with salt and pepper, to taste.
3. Heat an ovenproof skillet large enough to hold the beef over high heat; add 2 tablespoons vegetable oil and swirl to coat the bottom. When the pan is smoking, carefully place the beef in the skillet and sear on all sides, making a nice crust.
4. Place the skillet in the 400-degree oven to finish cooking to medium-rare or to your desired doneness. Check the meat with an instant read thermometer after 12 minutes. (See Internal Temperatures for Cooking Meat on page 7.)
5. Remove from the oven and allow to rest and cool. After about 30 minutes, thinly slice and place on a platter.

toppings

2 red bell peppers
2 yellow bell peppers
4 tablespoons vegetable oil
1 large red onion, julienned
Kosher salt and freshly ground black pepper, to taste

1. Preheat oven to 400 degrees.
2. Roast the whole peppers by tossing them with 2 table-spoons of the oil and then placing them on a sheet pan. Roast in the 400-degree oven for about 15 minutes. Check the peppers periodically. When they are blistered, remove them from the oven, place in a bowl and cover with plastic wrap to steam.
3. When the peppers are cool enough to handle, carefully remove their skins and seeds. Cut into strips and set aside.
4. Roast the onion. To do so, toss the pieces in a bowl with the remaining 2 tablespoons oil and season with salt and pepper, to taste.
5. Roast on a sheet pan in the 400-degree oven until tender (about 10 minutes), turning often to prevent burning. Remove from the oven and set aside.

basil pesto

2 cups packed fresh basil leaves
¼ cup pine nuts
2 cloves garlic
½ cup grated Parmesan cheese
½ cup extra-virgin olive oil
Kosher salt and freshly ground black pepper, to taste

1. Combine the basil, pine nuts, garlic and cheese in a food processor and pulse until coarsely chopped.
2. Add the oil and process until fully incorporated and smooth. Season with salt and pepper, to taste.

red wine vinaigrette

⅓ cup red wine vinegar
1 teaspoon sugar, or to taste
Kosher salt and freshly ground black pepper, to taste
1 tablespoon Dijon mustard
⅔ cup oil (half extra-virgin olive and half vegetable oil)

1. Whisk together all of the ingredients except oils.
2. Slowly drizzle in the oils, whisking constantly to emulsify. Set aside.

assembly

**1 loaf Asiago or another nice cheese bread, cut into
1-inch-thick slices (1-2 slices per person)**
Extra-virgin olive oil, as needed
1 bunch watercress, rinsed, tough stems removed
4 handfuls arugula
Kosher salt and freshly ground black pepper, to taste

1. Brush the bread slices with olive oil and grill on the stovetop in a grill pan until crisp.

2. Place 1-2 slices grilled bread on each plate; spread with the basil pesto. Layer each with a small handful of watercress, and a mixture of the peppers and red onion. Top with a couple slices beef (about 4 ounces per serving, 2 ounces per slice of grilled bread).

3. Place the arugula in a bowl and drizzle with the red wine vinaigrette; add salt and pepper, to taste. Toss and then place a portion on each plate with the bruschetta.

Serves 4

"Definitely use malt vinegar in th

Traditional Irish salad with cream dressing

We serve this salad at R bistro every year around St. Patrick's Day. The traditional presentation described below takes some time to compose, but the effort pays off. Definitely use malt vinegar in the dressing for the tang of flavor. I learned this dish while attending Balleymaloe Cookery School in Ireland.

Shanagarry cream dressing

2 eggs, hard-boiled
1 tablespoon soft brown sugar
1 pinch salt
1 teaspoon dried mustard
1 tablespoon brown malt vinegar
¼-½ cup heavy cream

1. Press the egg yolks through a sieve and chop the whites.

2. In a small mixing bowl, combine the sieved yolks with the brown sugar, salt and mustard. Stir in the vinegar and ¼ cup of the cream, adding another ¼ cup cream if needed to reach a smooth consistency. (Reserve the chopped whites for sprinkling over the salad.)

3. The dressing will keep covered and chilled for 24 hours.

salad beets

1 bunch beets, cleaned
½ cup sugar
1 cup water
½ cup white wine vinegar

1. Cook the beets in boiling water until a paring knife inserted into one comes out easily. Drain and allow to cool.

2. When the beets are cool enough to handle, peel them and cut into ¼-inch-thick slices. Place into a glass dish.

3. In a small saucepan over medium-low heat, dissolve the sugar in the water and stir in the vinegar. Remove from heat and pour over the beets; let them pickle for a few hours. (This can be done 1 day ahead of service.)

Irish salad

1-2 heads Bibb or Boston lettuce, leaves separated
1 bunch watercress, rinsed well, drained and stems trimmed
1 bunch radishes, quartered
1 English cucumber, peeled and cut into ¼-inch-thick slices
3 eggs, hard-boiled, peeled and quartered
1 bunch green onions, sliced into 2-inch pieces
½ pint grape tomatoes, halved
½ cup chopped fresh parsley, to garnish

1. Prepare all of the ingredients for the Irish salad. Have at the ready 4 dinner plates and 4 ramekins to hold the Shanagarry cream dressing.

2. Arrange the lettuce leaves on the 4 plates, using about 3-4 leaves per plate; they should be nice and fluffy. Divide the dressing among the ramekins and place 1 in the center of each plate on top of the lettuce leaves. Working around each ramekin, arrange the vegetables, starting with a small nosegay of watercress, and then about 3 radish quarters, 4 slices cucumber, 3 quarters egg, a few pieces green onion, 7 grape tomato halves and finish with 3 slices beet.

3. Garnish the dressing with chopped egg whites (reserved from making the dressing); sprinkle the plate with chopped parsley, to garnish. Enjoy the salad by dipping each vegetable into the Shanagarry cream dressing. (An alternative presentation appears in the photo on page 96.)

Serves 4

Pomegranate, orange and leaf salad tossed in raspberry dressing

This is a Christmas salad for sure! With the combination of pomegranate, orange and the green leaves, it will be perfect, tossed in our house raspberry vinaigrette.

raspberry vinaigrette

2 tablespoons granulated sugar
Kosher salt and white pepper, to taste
½ cup raspberry vinegar
½ cup water
1 cup salad oil (such as canola or grapeseed oil)
2 tablespoons finely chopped shallots

1. Combine all of the raspberry vinaigrette ingredients and mix well. This is not an emulsion, so the dressing will separate; whisk well before serving.

salad

1 pomegranate
2 oranges
Mixed lettuce leaves, as needed

1. Halve the pomegranate around the equator and, holding it over a bowl, carefully tap the skin with a spoon. The seeds should easily fall out. If they don't, remove the seeds individually; there should be no pith in the bowl. Set aside.

2. Using a small serrated knife, completely peel the oranges, removing the skin and all of the white pith. (You will end with total citrus.) To do so, over a bowl, take the peeled orange in your hand and run the knife down the membrane of a segment; cut down the segment's other opposite side, removing it intact. Do this completely around the orange, removing any seeds along the way. Squeeze any juice out of the remaining membranes into the bowl.

3. Set out 4 salad plates. Toss the leaves in a bowl with a little raspberry vinaigrette, enough to coat well, and place in the center of each plate. Place about 5-7 orange segments on the salad and then sprinkle with a handful of pomegranate seeds.

Serves 4

Parsnip and bacon cake with red pepper chutney

This is the perfect way to become familiar with parsnips, which have a sweet taste. This is a lovely combination of creamy parsnip cake topped with crispy bacon and then a dollop of red pepper chutney. Once you make this chutney, you'll want to try it with everything — sandwiches, pork, etc. The parsnip cake recipe is from Ireland, and the chutney recipe is from Elizabeth David, a British cookery writer from the mid-20th century.

red pepper chutney

½ **pound onions, finely chopped**
5 **tablespoons extra-virgin olive oil**
1 **pound red bell peppers, seeded and chopped**
½ **teaspoon salt**
½ **teaspoon powdered ginger or grated ginger root**
½ **teaspoon allspice**
½ **teaspoon mace**
½ **teaspoon nutmeg**
1 **pound Roma tomatoes, peeled and chopped**
¼ **pound golden raisins**
1 **clove garlic, chopped**
½ **pound white sugar**
1 **cup white wine vinegar**

1. In a stainless-steel saucepan, sweat the onions in the olive oil over medium heat.

2. Add the chopped peppers, salt and spices; stir and cook.

3. After 10 minutes, add the tomatoes, raisins, garlic, sugar and vinegar. Bring to a boil and simmer very gently until it looks thickish (about 1¼ hours).

4. Pour into a Kilner jar or other airtight jar, cool and then store in the refrigerator.

parsnip and bacon cakes

¼ **pound bacon, cut into ½-inch lardoons (pieces**
  cut crosswise)
Kosher salt, to taste
1 **pound parsnips, peeled and cut into chunks**
3 **tablespoons unsalted butter, or as needed**
Freshly ground black pepper, to taste
1 **cup all-purpose flour seasoned with salt and pepper**
1 **egg, beaten**
White bread crumbs, as needed
1 **tablespoon extra-virgin olive oil, or as needed**

1. In a saute pan, cook the bacon until crisp and drain on paper towels. Set aside.

2. Bring a pot of salted water and the parsnips to a boil. Reduce heat and simmer until tender when pierced with the tip of a knife (about 15 minutes). Drain well.

3. In a bowl, mash the parsnips with 2 tablespoons of the butter, and season with salt and pepper, to taste. Wet fingers and form 4 cakes (the moisture helps prevent sticking). Place on a plate.

4. Prepare a breading station, setting up separate dishes of seasoned flour, beaten egg and bread crumbs. Dip the cakes into the flour, being sure not to let it clump; and then in the egg; and then in the crumbs. Return the cakes to the plate and refrigerate for 10 minutes.

5. In a skillet large enough to hold all 4 cakes, bring 1 tablespoon olive oil and the remaining 1 tablespoon butter to bubbling over medium-high heat. Carefully place the cakes in the fat and brown on both sides until golden.

assembly

1. For each serving, place a freshly sauteed cake in the center of each plate. Garnish with the warm lardoons.

2. Top with the red pepper chutney.

Serves 4

"This is a wonderful Indian recipe for shrimp, but yo

Shrimp with spiced masala and coconut milk over basmati rice

This is a wonderful Indian recipe for shrimp, but you can use the sauce with chicken also. It's inspired by a recipe I found a few years ago in *Bon Appétit* and have been using ever since.

masala

2 tablespoons vegetable oil
2 cups chopped white onions
2 cloves garlic, chopped
1½ teaspoons garam masala
1½ teaspoons curry powder
1½ teaspoons ground coriander
1 teaspoon turmeric
½ teaspoon cayenne pepper
1 28-ounce can diced tomatoes, in juice
1 cup plain whole-milk yogurt
Kosher salt and freshly ground black pepper, to taste

1. Heat the oil in a large nonstick skillet over medium heat. Add the onions and saute until they are deep golden (about 20 minutes).

2. Add the garlic and all of the spices, stirring for 1 minute. Remove from heat and cool to lukewarm.

3. In a food processor or blender, puree the tomatoes with their juice and the yogurt until the mixture is almost smooth. Add the onion mixture and puree until almost smooth. Season the masala with salt and pepper, to taste. (This can be made 1 day ahead.)

shrimp

2 tablespoons vegetable oil
2 pounds large raw shrimp, peeled and deveined
1 13½-ounce can unsweetened coconut milk
½ cup chopped fresh cilantro
¼ cup chopped green onion tops
1½ tablespoons fresh lemon juice
Kosher salt and freshly ground black pepper, to taste

1. Heat the oil in a large heavy deep skillet over medium-high heat. Add the shrimp and saute until partially cooked (about 2 minutes). Stir in the coconut milk, cilantro, green onion tops, lemon juice and prepared masala. Simmer until the shrimp are opaque in the center (about 3 minutes longer). Season with salt and pepper, to taste.

basmati rice

Kosher salt, to taste
2 cups basmati rice
1 tablespoon unsalted butter
Freshly ground black pepper, to taste

1. Bring to a boil a large pot of salted water. Add the rice and stir. Cook the rice for 10 minutes and then drain in a colander. Cool under cold running water.

2. To serve, reheat in the microwave with the butter and salt and pepper, to taste.

assembly

Chopped fresh cilantro, to garnish

1. Divide the rice among 8 serving bowls, spooning it into the center. Ladle the shrimp masala on top of the rice, giving each person about 6 shrimp. Garnish with cilantro.

Serves 8

Hoisin five-spice chicken legs with warm Asian slaw

There are times when we need to come up with quick, easy ways to use chicken legs, both the thigh and drumstick. I found these hoisin legs and Asian slaw recipes on epicurious.com (*Gourmet*, March 2000) and thought they would pair well together. This is a really easy recipe.

chicken

4 chicken legs, thigh and drumstick separated
½ cup hoisin sauce
1 teaspoon Chinese five-spice powder

1. Preheat oven to 400 degrees.
2. Put the chicken in a shallow (1 inch deep) baking pan lined with foil.
3. Stir together the hoisin sauce and five-spice powder and brush liberally all over the chicken. Bake in the upper third of the 400-degree oven until the skin is browned, and the chicken is cooked through (25-30 minutes). (Allow the chicken to cool and set aside if not serving immediately. It can be reheated in the oven.)

dressing

1 tablespoon soy sauce
1 tablespoon cider vinegar
2 teaspoons Asian sesame oil
1½ teaspoons fresh minced ginger root
1½ teaspoons Asian chili paste
¼ cup creamy peanut butter
1 teaspoon sugar

1. Whisk together the dressing ingredients and set aside.

slaw

1 tablespoon vegetable oil
2 medium-size carrots, julienned
½ head cabbage, cut into ¼-inch-thick slices
½ cucumber, seeded and julienned

1. Heat the vegetable oil in a large heavy skillet over medium-high heat until hot but not smoking, and then saute the carrots, stirring frequently, until almost tender but not brown (about 2 minutes).

2. Add the cabbage and saute, stirring and tossing constantly, until wilted but still crisp tender (about 4 minutes).

3. Remove from heat and add the cucumber and dressing; toss well.

4. To serve, place the warm slaw in the center of each plate and top with 2 pieces of the warmed chicken (1 thigh and 1 drumstick).

Serves 4

White chicken chili

A recipe from *Gourmet* magazine that a girlfriend of mine gave me back in the early '90s inspired this chicken chili. I have made it at home and at the restaurant. It's delicious and not difficult at all.

½ **pound dried navy beans, picked over to remove any damaged beans**
1 **large white onion, chopped**
½ **cup (8 tablespoons) unsalted butter**
¼ **cup all-purpose flour**
¾ **cup chicken broth**
2 **cups half-and-half**
1 **teaspoon Tabasco red pepper sauce, or to taste**
1½ **teaspoons chili powder**
1 **teaspoon ground cumin**
½ **teaspoon kosher salt, or to taste**
½ **teaspoon white pepper, or to taste**
2 **jalapeños, seeds and stems removed, finely diced**
2 **pounds chicken tenders or breasts, cooked and cut into ½-inch pieces**
1½ **cups grated Monterey jack cheese (about 6 ounces)**
½ **cup sour cream**
Cilantro leaves, to garnish
Tomato salsa, to garnish *

1. Soak the beans in cold water overnight.

2. Drain them in a colander and place in a pot with fresh cold water to cover by 2 inches. Cook the beans at a bare simmer until tender (about 1 hour) and drain in a colander.

3. In a skillet, cook the onion in 2 tablespoons of the butter over medium heat until softened.

4. In a 6- to 8-quart heavy stockpot, melt the remaining 6 tablespoons butter over moderately low heat and whisk in the flour. Cook the roux, whisking constantly for 3 minutes. Stir in the onion and gradually add the broth and half-and-half, whisking constantly. Bring the mixture to a boil and then lower heat to a simmer, stirring occasionally, until thickened (about 5 minutes).

5. Stir in the Tabasco, chili powder, cumin, salt and white pepper. Add the beans, jalapeños, chicken and Monterey jack and cook the mixture over medium-low heat, stirring regularly, for 20 minutes. Stir the sour cream into the chili.

6. Garnish with cilantro and tomato salsa.

Serves 8

*To make a basic salsa, combine peeled, small-dice tomatoes; chopped cilantro; lime juice; chili peppers, such as jalapeños; salt and pepper; and chopped green onion. Adjust the seasonings, to taste.

Pan-seared Arctic char with Jerusalem artichokes and baby bok choy

This combination is very eye-catching, with the pink Arctic char, the creamy white color of the artichokes and then the brilliant bok choy. I worked with Jerusalem artichokes during the wintertime in England. This is a rich presentation of this vegetable. Out of California, they're called sunchokes.

Jerusalem artichokes/sunchokes

2 lemons, halved
About 3 pounds Jerusalem artichokes
Kosher salt, to taste
2 cups heavy cream
Freshly ground black pepper, to taste

1. Make a bath of acidulated water by filling a large bowl with water and the lemons. Carefully peel the artichokes and immediately place them in the water bath.

2. Drain the artichokes and place in a large pot of salted water. Bring to a boil. Cook until al dente (10-15 minutes). Drain well.

3. Slice the artichokes and slowly warm them up over medium-low heat with the cream in a pan. Season with salt and pepper, to taste. Cover to keep warm.

baby bok choy

4 bunches baby bok choy
Kosher salt, to taste
Unsalted butter, to taste
Freshly ground black pepper, to taste

1. Trim the ends of the bok choy and wash well.

2. Bring a saucepan of salted water to a boil over high heat. Drop the bok choy into the boiling water to blanch (1-3 minutes). Drain and shake off any excess water.

3. Over medium heat, toss the bok choy with butter, to taste, in a saute pan; add salt and pepper, to taste.

Arctic char

4 6-ounce filets Arctic char, trimmed, boned, skin on
Kosher salt and freshly ground black pepper, to taste
Vegetable oil, as needed

1. Season the filets on both sides with salt and pepper, to taste.

2. Heat a large skillet over high heat and add enough oil to just cover the bottom. When the pan is smoking hot, carefully place the filets in the oil, skin side down. Turn down the heat to medium-high and let the fish sear until the skin pulls away from the surface of the skillet (be patient). When the skin is crispy, and the fish is cooked about halfway through, turn the filets and finish cooking on the flesh side (until the inside is just opaque).

assembly

1. Set up 4 plates and place a spoonful of Jerusalem artichokes/sunchokes in the center of each plate. Angle the Arctic char against the artichokes, and angle the baby bok choy to the side of the char.

Serves 4

Pan-seared duck breast, sauteed kale and sweet potato cake with pomegranate sauce

The locally procured duck we serve at R bistro is from Maple Leaf Farms. We pan-sear the breasts, and our guests love it! Kale, a fairly unknown vegetable, comes alive here at the restaurant; we blanch it, refresh it in ice water, drain, squeeze and refrigerate. Each order is sauteed in butter, salt and pepper — delicious! The sweet potato cake presents well and is pretty basic for ingredients. The pomegranate sauce was adapted from a recipe from New York Chef Bobby Flay.

pan-seared duck breast

4 boneless duck breasts (5-8 ounces each)
1 tablespoon vegetable oil, or as needed
Kosher salt and freshly ground black pepper, to taste

1. Preheat oven to 400 degrees. Trim any silver skin or excess fat from the flesh side of the duck breasts. Turn over and score them on the fatty side using a very sharp knife, cutting about ⅛ inch into the skin in a diamond or cross-hatch pattern. Don't cut into the meat.

2. In a skillet large enough to hold 4 breasts, heat about 1 tablespoon vegetable oil over medium heat; swirl it in the pan. Season both sides of the breasts with salt and pepper, to taste. When the skillet is hot, carefully place the breasts into the pan, skin side down. Cook the duck until the skin is crispy, and the fat has rendered (6-8 minutes). Drain all but 1 tablespoon of the fat.

3. Turn the breasts over flesh side down and place them in the 400-degree oven 3-5 minutes for medium-rare duck. (See Internal Temperatures for Cooking Meat on page 7.) Remove from the oven and place on a cutting board; let rest for about 3 minutes. Slice each breast into 5 slices and fan.

kale

2 bunches kale (about 1½ pounds)
Kosher salt, to taste
4 tablespoons (½ stick) unsalted butter, plus more
  as needed
1 tablespoon extra-virgin olive oil
Freshly ground black pepper, to taste

1. Strip the kale leaves from their stems; discard stems. Rinse the leaves and place in a colander. Bring a large pot of salted water to a boil over high heat. Have an ice water bath at the ready.

2. Plunge the kale into the boiling water and blanch until the kale is al dente (4-6 minutes). Drain the kale and then immediately place in the ice water to stop the cooking process. Drain well, squeezing any excess water from the leaves.

3. In a large saute pan, place about half the butter and 1 tablespoon olive oil over medium-high heat. Add the kale and toss; season with salt and pepper, to taste. Add additional butter, if needed. Heat through, mixing with tongs.

mashed white potatoes

1 pound Idaho baking potatoes, peeled and cut into chunks
Kosher salt, to taste
3 tablespoons unsalted butter, cubed
Freshly ground black pepper, to taste
⅓ cup warm milk, or as needed

1. Place the potatoes in a pot with cold water (to cover) and salt, to taste. Bring to a boil over high heat and then reduce to a simmer.

2. Preheat oven to 400 degrees.

3. Cook the potatoes until they are fork tender. Drain them and then spread them out on a sheet tray. Place in the 400-degree oven for a few minutes to dry out.

4. Mash the potatoes with a potato masher, adding the butter and seasoning with salt and pepper, to taste.

5. Add the milk until you reach the desired consistency.

mashed sweet potatoes

1 pound sweet potatoes, scrubbed
1 tablespoon unsalted butter
Kosher salt and freshly ground black pepper, to taste

1. Preheat oven to 400 degrees.

2. Pierce the sweet potatoes with a fork. Bake them in a

(recipe continued on page 112)

(Pan-seared duck breast, sauteed kale and sweet potato cake with pomegranate sauce, continued from page 111)

roasting pan in the 400-degree oven until they are tender (45-60 minutes).

3. Cut the potatoes in half lengthwise. Being careful to protect your hands, scoop out the potato meat into a bowl and mash with a potato masher.

4. In a saucepan over medium heat, melt the butter. Remove from the heat and pour into the bowl of sweet potatoes. Stir to combine evenly. Season with salt and pepper, to taste.

sweet potato cake

1 onion, finely chopped
2 tablespoons unsalted butter
1 pound mashed white potatoes
1 pound mashed sweet potatoes
½ cup chopped fresh parsley
Kosher salt and freshly ground black pepper, to taste
½ cup all-purpose flour, or as needed
½ cup vegetable oil, or as needed

1. In a saute pan over medium heat, saute the onion in the butter until translucent. Remove from heat and allow to cool.

2. In a large mixing bowl, combine the white and sweet potatoes with the onion and parsley. Taste and adjust seasoning with salt and pepper.

3. Shape this mixture into 3-ounce cakes. Place the completed cakes on a parchment-lined sheet tray. (These can be refrigerated until ready to saute.)

4. Pour about ½ cup flour onto a plate. Dip each cake in the flour and return to the sheet tray.

5. Bring a skillet large enough to hold all 4 cakes to medium-high heat, and then add about ½ cup vegetable oil. When the oil is hot, carefully place the cakes in the skillet and cook until golden brown on both sides, adjusting heat so that they do not burn. (Any additional cakes can be used later for a breakfast side or a midnight snack.)

pomegranate sauce

1½ cups orange juice
1½ cups pomegranate juice (bottled or fresh)
¼ cup port
1 cup red wine
1 large shallot, chopped
1 carrot, chopped
1 stalk celery, chopped
1 cup chicken stock
4 black peppercorns
4 sprigs parsley
1 bay leaf
2 tablespoons cold unsalted butter
Kosher salt and freshly ground pepper, to taste

1. Place all of the ingredients except the butter, salt and pepper in a medium-size saucepan and cook until reduced to a sauce consistency.

2. Strain and whisk in the cold butter. Season with salt and pepper, to taste.

assembly

1. Place the kale on each of 4 plates. Angle the sweet potato cake against the kale and fan the warm duck breast on the cake. Drizzle a little of the pomegranate sauce on the duck and on the plate.

Serves 4

Baked potato salad with chipotle butter and spicy black bean and corn salad

Here is a totally vegetarian way to present a baked potato. This black bean and corn salad has been around here at R bistro from the beginning. I used to serve it with broiled halibut and mango salsa. It's just a basic combination of ingredients that pair well together.

red wine vinaigrette

⅓ cup red wine vinegar
2 seeded, minced jalapeños
Kosher salt and freshly ground black pepper, to taste
Sugar, to taste
⅔ cup extra-virgin olive oil

1. Whisk all of the ingredients together or process in a blender until combined. Adjust to your taste.

spicy black bean and corn salad

2 cups dried black beans
1 tablespoon cumin seeds
About 1 tablespoon salt, plus more to taste
3 cups fresh corn kernels (or frozen, thawed)
½ red onion, small dice
1 bunch green onions, white and green parts chopped
½ bunch cilantro, chopped
2 cups peeled and chopped tomatoes

1. Rinse the beans well under cold running water. Drain and place in a saucepan. Add water to cover, bring to a boil over high heat and boil for 2 minutes. Remove from the heat and cover. Let stand for 1 hour and then drain.

2. Return the beans to the saucepan and add enough water to cover them by about 3 inches. Place over high heat and bring to a boil. Cover the saucepan with a lid slightly ajar; reduce heat to low and simmer for about 30 minutes.

3. Stir the cumin seeds into the beans. Continue cooking until the beans are tender but still hold their shape (about 40 minutes longer). When they are just done, add the salt and stir. Drain well and allow them to cool.

4. In a large bowl, combine the black beans and all of the remaining ingredients except tomatoes and toss with enough vinaigrette to coat.

5. Add the tomatoes and toss gently. Adjust seasoning with salt, to taste.

potatoes

8 baking potatoes, washed and scrubbed well
Vegetable oil, as needed
Kosher salt and freshly ground black pepper, to taste

1. Preheat oven to 400 degrees. Rub the potato skins with oil and season with salt and pepper, to taste. Punch a few fork holes into the skin to allow steam to escape during cooking.

2. Bake the potatoes directly on the rack in the 400-degree oven until fork tender (about 1 hour).

chipotle butter

½ pound unsalted butter, room temperature
1 chipotle pepper in adobo, chopped
Kosher salt, to taste

1. Using a mixer, soften and blend the butter.

2. Add the chopped chipotle with a little adobo sauce and salt, to taste. Do not make it too spicy, but blend well.

3. Divide the butter into 2 pieces and place on parchment paper. Roll each piece into a 1½-inch-wide log. Freeze and cut slices as needed.

assembly

Mixed salad leaves, as needed
Kosher salt and freshly ground black pepper, to taste

1. Toss the salad leaves in a bowl with enough red wine vinaigrette to coat and then place in the center of each individual plate.

2. Cut an X in the top of each potato and place a slice of chipotle butter inside. Season the potato with salt and pepper, to taste. Place it on the leaves and then top with the spicy black bean and corn salad.

Serves 8

Spiced pork tenderloin with celery root puree and French lentils

This recipe was inspired by a wonderful combination of *Bon Appétit* magazine recipes from a few years back. I've served it at the restaurant for dinner as well as for special parties. I even taught a cooking class with it. The three-part combination fits well together and tastes great.

celery root puree

2 pounds (1-2 heads) celeriac (celery root), peeled and cut into 2-inch cubes
5 cups whole milk
2 tablespoons unsalted butter
1 teaspoon fresh lemon juice
Kosher salt and white pepper, to taste

1. Bring the celeriac and milk to a boil in a large heavy saucepan over high heat. Reduce heat and simmer uncovered until the celeriac is very tender (about 20 minutes).

2. Using a slotted spoon, transfer the celeriac to a food processor. Add ½ cup of the hot milk. Puree until the mixture is very smooth.

3. Blend in the butter and lemon juice. Season with salt and white pepper, to taste. Keep warm.

lentils

3 bacon slices, chopped
¼ cup ⅛-inch cubes peeled carrot
¼ cup chopped shallots
¼ teaspoon minced fresh rosemary
1½ cups dried French lentils
3 cups water
1 teaspoon unsalted butter
Kosher salt and freshly ground black pepper, to taste

1. Saute the bacon in a medium-size saucepan over medium-high heat until crisp (about 3 minutes).

2. Add the carrot, shallots and rosemary; saute until the shallots begin to soften (about 1 minute).

3. Add the lentils and 3 cups water; bring to boil. Reduce the heat and simmer uncovered until the lentils are tender, and the liquid has nearly evaporated (about 35 minutes). Stir in the butter. Season with salt and pepper, to taste.

pork tenderloin

½ cup honey
6 tablespoons red wine vinegar
1 tablespoon curry powder
½ teaspoon cayenne pepper, or to taste
Vegetable oil, as needed
2½ pounds pork tenderloin, trimmed
Kosher salt and freshly ground black pepper, to taste
¾ cup chicken broth
1 tablespoon cold unsalted butter

1. Whisk together the honey, red wine vinegar, curry powder and cayenne pepper in a bowl.

2. Preheat oven to 400 degrees.

3. Rub oil into the pork. Season the meat with salt and pepper, to taste. Mark the pork on all sides on a char broiler or in a hot, ovenproof saute pan over medium-high heat. Brush the pork with the honey mixture (reserving the leftover mixture) and place in an ovenproof saute pan. Cook the meat in the 400-degree oven until an instant-read thermometer reads 150 degrees. (See Internal Temperatures for Cooking Meat on page 7.) Transfer the pork to a work surface.

4. Make a sauce by deglazing the pan with the chicken broth and a spoonful of the honey mixture, scraping up any bits stuck to the pan. Boil the sauce over high heat until it is reduced. Whisk in a little chilled butter and adjust the seasonings, to taste. Keep warm.

assembly

1. Warm the celeriac puree and lentils. Slice the pork tenderloin into ½-inch-thick slices. Place ½ cup celeriac puree in the center of each of 6 plates; make an indentation in the puree. Spoon ½ cup of the lentils into each well. Arrange the pork slices atop the lentils and drizzle with sauce. (An alternative presentation appears in the photo on page 114.)

Serves 6

"During the winter months, we enjoye

My mum's veal and tomatoes with elbow macaroni

Growing up, we normally had this dish in late summer when the garden was full of green peppers and tomatoes at their peak. During the winter, we enjoyed my mum's canned tomatoes in this dish. I have changed it a little by adding fresh basil at the end of cooking and a touch of tomato paste to thicken if necessary. It reminds me of the summer, just as school would be starting back for the year.

2 pounds cubed veal
Kosher salt and freshly ground black pepper, to taste
4-5 tablespoons extra-virgin olive oil, or as needed
3 green peppers, seeded and sliced
2 large onions, roughly chopped
3 cloves garlic, chopped
2 quarts tomatoes, peeled and quartered (about 6-7 pounds fresh tomatoes make 2 quarts canned tomatoes)
½ teaspoon sugar
1 teaspoon dried basil
1 teaspoon dried Italian seasoning (such as McCormick or grocery store brand)
1 pound elbow macaroni
Tomato paste, as needed
2 tablespoons fresh basil chiffonade (cut into ribbon-like strips)
2 tablespoons chopped fresh parsley

1. Generously season the veal with salt and pepper, to taste.

2. Heat about 3 tablespoons of the olive oil in a large pan over medium-high heat. Brown the meat in the hot oil in batches (adding more oil as needed); remove the browned veal to a plate and set aside.

3. To the same pan, add the peppers, onions and garlic (being careful not to burn the garlic). Cook the vegetables until the peppers and onions are tender. This will take at least 15 minutes.

4. Add the meat back to the pan along with the tomatoes and their juices, sugar and dried herbs. Combine well and season with salt and pepper, to taste. Reduce heat to low and cook for about 2 hours, covered. The liquid will cook down, and the veal will be very tender.

5. While the veal mixture is cooking, cook the elbow macaroni until it is al dente, according to package directions. Drain and toss in a little olive oil so the macaroni won't stick; keep warm.

6. Check the sauce for thickness. You may need to add tomato paste to thicken it. Adjust seasonings and stir in the fresh basil and parsley.

7. To serve, place the warmed elbows in serving bowls. Top each bowl with a ladleful of veal and tomatoes. Garnish with chopped parsley.

Serves 5-6 generously

Pistachio semifreddo with chocolate sauce

This recipe is adapted from one I found in the January 2007 issue of *Gourmet* magazine. I was intrigued with the fact that there were only five ingredients and I love pistachios, so I tried it. It's not difficult to make and presents beautifully. Warm chocolate sauce and toasted pistachios dress it well.

pistachio semifreddo

1½ cups shelled salted pistachios
1 cup sugar
6 egg whites
2 cups cold heavy cream
¼ teaspoon almond extract

1. In a food processor, pulse 1 cup of the pistachios with ½ cup plus 2 tablespoons of the sugar until the nuts are very finely ground. Add the remaining ½ cup pistachios and pulse until just coarsely ground.

2. Using an electric mixer at medium speed, in a large mixing bowl beat the egg whites until they hold soft peaks. Continue beating and gradually add in the remaining ¼ cup plus 2 tablespoons sugar. Increase the mixer speed to high and beat until the meringue holds stiff peaks.

3. In a separate bowl, beat the cream with the almond extract at high speed until it just holds soft peaks.

4. Carefully fold the meringue into the cream until they are completely integrated; fold in the nut mixture in the same manner. Spoon the mixture into a terrine lined with plastic wrap and freeze, covered, until it's firm enough to scoop (about 4 hours).

chocolate sauce

1 cup heavy cream
7 ounces fine-quality bittersweet chocolate, finely chopped

1. While the semifreddo is freezing, make the chocolate sauce by bringing the heavy cream to a boil over high heat in a small saucepan.

2. Place the chocolate in the bottom of a mixing bowl. When the cream is boiling, remove it from the heat and pour over the chocolate; stir to melt the chocolate and combine well.

assembly

Shelled salted pistachios, to garnish

1. Preheat oven to 400 degrees. Place the pistachios on a small sheet tray. Toast the nuts in the 400-degree oven until golden. Check after 3 minutes and watch carefully until lightly toasted. Remove from the oven, allow to cool and chop.

2. Let the semifreddo soften slightly before serving. To serve, slice and serve with chocolate sauce and toasted chopped pistachios.

Yields 2 quarts

Red velvet cake with buttercream icing

This is my birthday cake. I was born the day before Valentine's Day, so when I was little Mum or Aunt Maude would bake me a red cake for my birthday. Since I've had the restaurant, I've had red velvet cake on the menu every year during Valentine's week. It has been quite a hit with the guests, even if they don't know it's my birthday. I make sure I have a slice every night after work. I have had this recipe for years; I'm not sure where Mum got it, probably from some lady friend.

cake

½ cup unsalted butter, room temperature
1½ cups sugar
2 eggs, room temperature
2 level teaspoons unsweetened cocoa powder
2 ounces red food coloring
1 teaspoon salt
1 teaspoon vanilla extract
1 cup buttermilk
2 cups all-purpose flour
1½ teaspoons baking soda
1 teaspoon vinegar

1. Spray 2 8-inch cake pans with Baker's Joy nonstick spray. Preheat oven to 350 degrees.

2. In a mixing bowl, cream together the butter, sugar and eggs. Add the cocoa powder and food coloring, mixing in well.

3. In a small bowl, mix the salt with the vanilla; add this to buttermilk in another bowl.

4. Alternating the buttermilk mixture and flour, gradually add these to the creamed mixture.

5. In a small bowl, mix together the baking soda and vinegar; gently fold this into the batter (do not beat).

6. Pour the batter into the 2 prepared pans and bake in the 350-degree oven for 30 minutes or until a toothpick inserted in the middle comes out clean. Allow the cakes to cool before removing from the pans.

frosting

5 tablespoons all-purpose flour
1 cup milk
1 cup unsalted butter, softened
1 cup sugar
2 teaspoons vanilla extract

1. Whisk the flour and milk in a saucepan over medium heat until smooth. Bring to a boil; cook and stir for 2 minutes or until the mixture has thickened. Remove from heat, cover and refrigerate.

2. In a mixing bowl, cream the butter and sugar. Add the chilled mixture to this, beating for 10 minutes or until the frosting is fluffy. Stir in the vanilla.

assembly

1. Frost the cake between the layers, on the top and around the sides.

Serves 8-10

Recipe list by name

Index

Berries

Blackberry pie with vanilla ice cream, 57

Lamb and feta quesadilla with **lingonberry** and toasted hazelnut salsa, 92

Strawberry and mango sable, 27

Broccoli

Italian chicken cutlet with orzo and **broccoli**, 18

Celery root

Spiced pork tenderloin with **celery root puree** and French lentils, 115

Cheese

Asparagus, red pepper and **goat cheese** salad, 13

Broiled Alaskan halibut on a lentil salad with sliced tomatoes and **feta**, 45

Chicken breast topped with warm mushrooms, leeks and **goat cheese** over dressed mixed greens, 77

Filet of beef with spring fava beans and radishes and **French feta cheese**, 25

Indiana watermelon with prosciutto de Parma and **Gorgonzola**, 33

Lamb and **feta** quesadilla with lingonberry and toasted hazelnut salsa, 92

Meatballs with ricotta in broth with green sauce, 85

Pâté of the South: **pimento cheese** and house-made flatbread, 64

Quail and sausage braised with grapes, with **blue cheese** and walnut polenta, 79

Roasted red pepper stuffed with green and wax beans, **feta cheese** and kalamata olives, 37

Corn

Baked potato salad with chipotle butter and spicy black bean and **corn** salad, 113

Indiana beefsteak tomato stuffed with **Cobb salad**, 51

Ruby red trout with **wild rice succotash** and Pernod sauce, 73

Desserts

Blackberry pie with vanilla ice cream, 57

My mother's cheesecake, 89

Peach praline pie with vanilla ice cream, 59

Pistachio semifreddo with chocolate sauce, 119

Red velvet cake with buttercream icing, 121

Strawberry and mango sable, 27

Toffeed apple and pecan tart, 87

Greens, cooking

Marinated lamb T-bones with Himalayan red rice and **sauteed broccoli rabe**, 23

Pan-seared Arctic char with Jerusalem artichokes and **baby bok choy**, 109

Pan-seared duck breast, **sauteed kale** and sweet potato cake with pomegranate sauce, 111

Sumac-rubbed loin of lamb with flageolet beans, 81

Vegetable Wellington with **Swiss chard**, 39

Jerusalem artichokes

Pan-seared Arctic char with **Jerusalem artichokes** and baby bok choy, 109

Lamb

Lamb and feta quesadilla with lingonberry and toasted hazelnut salsa, 92

Marinated lamb T-bones with Himalayan red rice and sauteed broccoli rabe, 23

Sumac-rubbed loin of lamb with flageolet beans, 81

Leeks

Chicken breast topped with warm mushrooms, **leeks** and goat cheese over dressed mixed greens, 77

Turkey meatloaf with **leek mash** and green beans, 20

Mango

Prosciutto de Parma over a salad of **mango**, cucumber and fennel, 14

Strawberry and **mango** sable, 27

Mixed Vegetables

Filet of beef with **spring fava beans and radishes** and French feta cheese, 25

Grilled veal chops with **vegetable hash and horseradish**, 83

Meatballs with ricotta in **broth** with green sauce, 85

Pasta primavera, 17

Porcini-crusted New York strip steak with **summer vegetables**, 55

Prosciutto-wrapped Alaskan halibut on **panzanella**, 47

Roasted red pepper stuffed with **green and wax beans**, feta cheese and kalamata olives, 37

Ruby red trout with **wild rice succotash** and Pernod sauce, 73

Smoked trout with **red onion, cucumber and tomato salad**, 43

Succotash atop a zucchini pancake and sliced tomatoes, 35

Traditional Irish salad with cream dressing, 97

Vegetable Wellington with Swiss chard, 39

Mushrooms

Chicken breast topped with **warm mushrooms**, leeks and goat cheese over dressed mixed greens, 77

Oranges

Pomegranate, **orange** and leaf salad tossed in raspberry dressing, 98

Parsnip

Parsnip and bacon cake with red pepper chutney, 101

Pasta/Grains

Broiled Alaskan halibut on a **lentil salad** with sliced tomatoes and feta, 45

Chili-honey glazed shrimp over **brown rice with black beans**, 70

Italian chicken cutlet with **orzo** and broccoli, 18

Marinated lamb T-bones with **Himalayan red rice** and sauteed broccoli rabe, 23

My mum's veal and tomatoes with **elbow macaroni**, 117

Pasta primavera, 17

Quail and sausage braised with grapes, with blue cheese and walnut **polenta**, 79

Ruby red trout with **wild rice succotash** and Pernod sauce, 73

Shrimp with spiced masala and coconut milk over **basmati rice**, 103

Spiced pork tenderloin with celery root puree and **French lentils**, 115

Peaches

Peach, almond, Parmesan and mixed leaf salad tossed in **champagne-peach dressing**, 30

Peach praline pie with vanilla ice cream, 59

Pomegranates

Pan-seared duck breast, sauteed kale and sweet potato cake with **pomegranate sauce**, 111

Pomegranate, orange and leaf salad tossed in raspberry vinaigrette, 98